Last Minute Study Tips

By
Ron Fry

CAREER PRESS
3 Tice Road
P.O. Box 687
Franklin Lakes, NJ 07417
1-800-CAREER-1
201-848-0310 (NJ and outside U.S.)
FAX: 201-848-1727

LAST MINUTE STUDY TIPS

Cover design by Foster & Foster

Printed in the U.S.A. by Book-mart Press

To order this title by mail, please include price as noted above, $2.50 handling per order, and $1.00 for each book ordered. Send to: Career Press, Inc., 3 Tice Road, P.O. Box 687, Franklin Lakes, NJ 07417.

Or call toll-free 1-800-CAREER-1 (NJ and Canada: 201-848-0310) to order using VISA or MasterCard, or for further information on books from Career Press.

Library of Congress Cataloging-in-Publication Data

Fry, Ronald W.
Last minute study tips / by Ron Fry.
p. cm.
Includes index.
ISBN 1-56414-238-8
1. Study skills. 2. Students--Time management. I. Title.
LB1049.F737 1996
371.3'028'12--dc20 96-7624
CIP

Contents

Introduction

This book is written for everyone who has to make the most of the study time available. The ideas it outlines will be of benefit to you whether you are a high school student, a college student, an adult in school—or an instructor who is eager to *help* students get the most done with their time.

The techniques you'll find outlined in this book are targeted toward those who have very little time to spare. Because time is at a premium in the current volume, I have offered concise reviews of some of the most important topics of interest to students. For an in-depth review of note-taking, time management, reading comprehension, memory improvement and a host of other subjects dealt with here, please check your bookstore for the appropriate title in the ***How to Study*** series. These books are available individually at retail bookstores, or as a set by calling 1-800-CAREER-1.

My aim in outlining the "accelerated" study techniques discussed in this book is a simple one: To help you make the most of the time at your disposal—and to help you *learn* the most from the material you're studying. I hope the techniques you're about to discover help you to attain those worthy objectives.

—Ron Fry

Chapter 1

Your prime time

A worst-case scenario

Jane had always been a "morning person"—and as midterms approached during her freshman year, she usually spent the early morning hours before her classes hooking her laptop computer up to the Internet and catching up on the latest discussions in the chat groups she'd found there. One group was devoted entirely to discussions of Jane's favorite band, and she'd become quite popular there.

The truth was, she'd actually become close to some of the friends she'd made online...and she thought her discussions with them provided a good counterpoint to the studying she'd been doing in the evening at the library. And the more she studied, it seemed, the more she needed *that counterpoint—because the hours at the library seemed to drag on, and the material she was reading (from a favorite class!) just didn't seem to be sticking.*

After four weeks of this routine, Jane realized the night before her midterm exam that she was completely unprepared for the test she would have to take the next day.

Your prime time is *yours*—spend it wisely!

If you're reading this book, it's a good bet that you or someone you know is interested in getting a whole lot of good study work done in a very short period of time. To a large degree, the key to making the very most out of your day lies in knowing *when you get your best work done* and then acting on that knowledge.

All of this boils down to a single question, one you should consider closely before you move ahead in this book. Is your "kick-back" time scheduled at the *wrong* time?

To get the most out of the ideas that follow in this book, you should develop a sense for when your own peak times—the times when you are likely to be most effective, most enthusiastic and most detail-oriented—typically arise.

So, take a brief moment now to chart what you feel to be your most productive and satisfying time periods during the course of an average day.

On a separate piece of paper, write down, from memory, a rough guess at what you did when over the last couple of days. (If you prefer, you can jot down the details of a period of time that seems more relevant to you, such as a volunteer job or an extended period of study at the library.) Just for now, focus on both study and work issues *and* your other activities. Write down *everything* you did, as best you can recall.

As a general rule, when were you happiest and most upbeat during the course of the day? When were you "stuck in neutral"? When did it seem as though you couldn't manage to get much of *anything* done? If you're like most people, you'll find that you have good times and not-so-good times for tackling projects.

In my case, I'm an evening person. The hours between 4 p.m. and 11:30 p.m. are my prime time. It's not that I *can't* take on a project at 2 in the afternoon, but it so happens that, thanks to my own particular body chemistry, mind-set and accumulated habits, evenings are the time I feel best about doing what I'm doing. That's when I get the most done. That's when the quality of my work tends to be the best. That's when I have to be most careful about pointing my energy toward "leisure activities" (like surfing the Internet) that have an unpleasant habit of sucking all the initiative out of a day.

That's my pattern. It may not be the same as yours, but I'd venture to guess that you do have *some* pattern that corresponds to it.

If you're trying to get a lot done at the last minute in your studies, it is absolutely imperative that you know and, whenever possible, take advantage of your own personal "prime-time" patterns.

Many a poor grade can be traced back to poor personal scheduling. In this case, I'm not talking about the type of poor scheduling where someone scolds you about how you should have started a paper a couple of weeks ago. I'm *assuming* you've put off whatever you have to do until just before it's due—and, because this state of affairs has brought you to these pages, I've got no problem with that looming deadline! (Personally, I think a lot of people get their best work done when they are forced to focus their attentions just before a due date.) No, the poor personal scheduling I'm talking about is the kind that *doesn't let you take advantage of your own personal "prime time."*

If you're a "morning person"—that is to say, if you generally feel strongest, most in control and most active before the noon hour—you are doing yourself and your grades a disservice if you spend that time on nonstudy activities and then try to "buckle down" in the afternoon, the evening or, God forbid, past midnight. If you don't schedule your day in a way that allows you to focus on your studies during your peak hours, *you're trying to do your best work at the wrong time.* You're likely to remember less, write more poorly and make fewer of the critical connections necessary to attain a good grade.

If you're a "midday person"—that is to say, if you generally feel strongest, most in control and most active after noon but before 5 p.m.—you are doing yourself and your grades a disservice if you spend that time on nonstudy activities and then try to make up for it by downing a few cups of coffee to pull you through the sluggish evening (or morning) hours. You must work to schedule your study day in a way that allows you to focus your efforts during your peak hours—otherwise *you'll be trying to do your best work at the wrong time.*

It's important for you to manage classroom and work commitments in a way that allows you to take advantage of whatever portion of peak time you can claim during the course of the day. If you don't, your memory won't be working at peak efficiency, your writing skills will suffer, and your ability to draw conclusions and make connections will be less impressive than it should be.

If you're an "evening person"—that is to say, if you generally feel strongest, most in control and most active after 5 p.m. or so—you will not be performing up to your full capacity unless you find some way to take advantage of your ability to do study work at this time of the day. For you, the occasional late-night session may make a good deal of sense. If you let work, classroom or social commitments affect your schedule in such a way that the bulk of your study and research time is concentrated in the morning hours or the first half of the day, *you will be trying to get your best work done at the wrong time.* Know your cycles and peak performance times, and schedule accordingly. If you don't, you'll likely have problems remembering key points, your ability to compose text for reports won't be as strong as it should be, and you won't be making the key connections and parallels that will help you win good grades.

Please don't proceed any further in this book until you've taken the time to review your own personal schedule over the past few days (or any other period of time that seems appropriate to you) and *identified—or made an informed guess at—your personal prime time during the day.*

One more point about *you*

In the next two chapters, we'll start reviewing the essential time management and study skills you'll need to do the best possible job—within a limited time frame—when it comes to test preparation and writing papers. *The next two chapters contain important ideas that will help you through the rest of the program, so don't skip them.* If you don't read Chapters 2 and 3, you won't understand much of what we'll be discussing in Chapters 4 through 12.

You will need a clear head, a full stomach and an unshakable commitment to the project if you hope to get the grade you deserve. Don't put yourself at a disadvantage! Stay away from drugs and alcohol. Eat right. Don't get distracted with social or other activities that are not study-related during this, your "crunch time." Clear the decks and focus with your full, undivided attention on the matter at hand.

Now, let me make an important point before we proceed. Sometimes you can rearrange your schedule to take full advantage of your "prime time." And sometimes you can't. If you determine that you work most effectively between 1 and 5 p.m., but you have work commitments that occupy that time period, you have a couple of options. You can try to rearrange your work schedule on a temporary basis, or you can make the best use of the available time that is *closest to your prime time.*

Whether or not you can clear away a slot that will allow you to take advantage of your "prime time," you must make a commitment to devote an appropriate amount of your *available* time to your study tasks. If that means making the most of a 25-minute stretch between work and class commitments, so be it. You must make a commitment to use the time that is available to you, and you must use it wisely.

If you've got serious time pressures on the study front, your best option is to *identify and utilize your "prime time."* That's when you'll work most effectively, and working effectively is what it's all about when you're talking about tight deadlines.

If your "prime time" is occupied with work-related or class-related commitments that cannot be shifted on a temporary basis, your *next best option* is to identify and utilize the available slot closest to your "prime time."

If *nothing* near your "prime time" slot is available to you, *deciding not to study is not an option!* Working when you are at your peak is an important goal, but it is not always one we can attain. Resolve to make the most of the time that is available to you! Don't fall into the trap of "waiting until you are in the right mind-set"—and therefore putting the project off. This will only make your scheduling problems worse.

Do the best you can with the time that you can make for yourself. But *know* what your "prime time" is—and don't let it slip away. During times of tight scheduling and intense activity, being able to make full use of the best hours of your day is one of your most powerful weapons.

If you've got a handle on what constitutes your "prime time" during the course of the day, you're ready to take advantage of the ideas that follow in this book. Let's go!

Chapter 2

Some essential time management skills

No matter how late you are, you *do* have enough time to plan

Okay, you've *tried* to clear the decks and find some time to commit to that imminent test or report. But it's not a *lot* of time. And let's be realistic: you do have other commitments—classes, work schedules, occasionally talking to other human beings in a social setting and maybe even watching a television show every once in a while. Perhaps you've put this project off for a while, and that means your time is tight. Doesn't it make sense to just start in on the project and get whatever you can done? At least you'll finish *something* that way. Why not just open the book and start cramming?

Don't do it.

You *always* benefit by taking a little time—and in some situations that may be a *very* little time—to plan your attack. The condensed time management program you're about to learn is flexible; it will help you make choices about what's important in your situation, set goals for yourself and develop an organized, logical approach to your study task, one that helps you develop self-discipline and the motivation you'll need to complete your task successfully.

Read this chapter and the one that follows about some simple steps you can take to quickly improve your memory, *before you proceed to the subsequent chapters of this book.* If you don't take advantage of the advice here about time management, and the advice in the following chapter on *mnemonic* (memory-boosting) techniques, you won't be able to follow the program in its entirety.

Your battle plan

If you want to go grocery shopping, you need to make a list. If you want to get a good job, you need a realistic career goal, an intelligently selected list of prospective employers and a series of workable strategies for reaching those employers. If you want to study and achieve a good grade, you need a battle plan.

Mind you, it's *possible* to go shopping without a grocery list. You'll probably spend more than you should, and you may forget several important items, but you *can* do it. It's also *possible* to go looking for any job that happens to come your way. Lots of people do just that, and their job searches tend to last a lot longer than they should and land them in positions that really aren't that satisfying.

And you certainly *can* study for an imminent test or paper by simply opening your book to a sympathetic-looking page and reading until something that seems worth remembering materializes. But wouldn't you rather leave that to someone else? Wouldn't you rather *their* grades came in at a subpar level?

This program will show you how to spend a *small fraction* of your total study time identifying key time management goals, and then use the rest of your available time much more efficiently as a result. The exciting, all-too-often neglected truth is this: The amount of *time* you spend studying is far less important than how *effective* you make your study work. Making a modest time investment up front will allow you to develop an intelligent, flexible plan that will work for you...and help you hit that impending completion date with your very best effort.

Study Plan Central

Let's get started. You will need to find a notebook or diary that will serve one and only purpose: *recording all your schedule information.*

You can use anything you want, with as much or as little scheduling-related layout inside as you feel is appropriate. But make a commitment to making this book Study Plan Central. This book is going to serve as your repository for critical information, including:

- Project due dates.
- Class times.
- Study schedules you develop.
- Meetings you schedule.
- Nonstudy commitments.
- Vacations.

Personalize, personalize!

Which time management approach is "right"? The one that works the best for you. The one you feel most comfortable with. The one you can customize to your habits and predispositions. That's the beautiful thing about your Study Plan Central book. As long as it contains the information just outlined, as long as you take the book everywhere you go and as long as you give the book *daily* attention and enter everything into it *on a regular basis*—you can point the system in pretty much any direction you want!

Now, there *are* some essential, easy-to-customize tools you can use in this notebook, and we'll be looking at them in a moment. But before we do that, please remember the following points, without which the tools you incorporate in your Study Plan Central book aren't going to do you much good at all!

The three keys to long-term time management success:

1. Enter all time- and schedule-related information in your Study Plan Central book.
2. Take the book with you everywhere you go.
3. Give the book regular, daily attention and write things down in it on a regular basis.

Have you ever had this experience? You miss an important meeting or appointment and later say to yourself, "I know I had that written down *somewhere.*" If you follow the system outlined in this chapter, your Study Plan Central book will remove that problem for you—permanently.

You'll find some sample time management forms on pages 21 to 23 that you can photocopy and incorporate into your Study Plan Central book.

First, you'll find a *Planning Calendar,* which you should *enlarge dramatically with your photocopier* and use to record all the time essentials of your academic projects and your daily life. And I mean *everything.* Start with your due date and work backwards, including all the intermediary steps related to your project you know about. Write down all your relevant work commitments. Write down all your personal commitments. It won't take long, so why not invest a few minutes now? You'll find an example of a filled-out Planning Calendar on page 21.

After the Planning Calendar, you'll find a weekly *Priority Task Sheet.* This will help you arrange your tasks in *order of importance*—which is, I assure you, *not* necessarily the order in which they show up! Intelligent use of your Priority Task Sheet every week is an absolute must if you are facing a last-minute study situation.

How do you use the sheet? Write down everything you want to get done over the next week. Then ask yourself, "If I can only get one or two things done this week, what would they be?" Write these down and mark them with an "H." These are the urgent, high-priority items. Now ask yourself which of the things could conceivably wait until *next* week. These are the low-priority items; mark them with an "L." (By the way, if you find yourself putting off something in this category week after week, take a moment to consider whether you should really be focusing on it at all!) Everything else is a middle-priority. Mark it with an "M." You'll find an example of a completed Priority Task Sheet on page 22.

The last form you'll be working with is the *Daily Schedule.* Before you enter *anything* onto this schedule of an academic or work-related nature, remember the essentials! You have to eat. You have to sleep. Once you've built these basics into your day, you'll be ready to transfer the items from your Priority Task Sheet to your Daily Schedule. Put the items marked with an "H" first; whenever you can, put the most intimidating or difficult tasks *first.* (Give them your best shot, then get them out of the way!) Then enter as many "M" items as you can realistically fit into the day. Finally, enter any of the "L" items there's enough room in the schedule to accommodate.

So—let's say you have three hours free on Wednesday afternoon. As luck would have it, afternoons are your personal "prime time," so you want to make the very most of this block of time. You schedule your "H"-priority research-gathering work for that slot, and you plan to start that sociology assignment, due next month, between breakfast and your 10 a.m. class. However you manage your day, be sure to *update your Daily Schedule every single day!* An example of a completed Daily Schedule appears on page 23.

Blank copies of all three of these essential forms appear at the end of this chapter. Copy as many of them as your situation demands and incorporate them into your personal Study Plan Central notebook!

"So what else do I need besides the Study Plan Central book?"

The rest of the time management system you'll be using can be boiled down to 10 basic principles—the 10 commandments, if you will, of good time management:

1. **Find a place to study where you won't be interrupted.** For some people, it's the nearest library; for others, it's a desk or card table in a secluded corner of their home. Whatever pleasant, distraction-free environment you select, you should find a specific place and designate it as the place where studying, and nothing but studying, occurs. Make sure all the materials you need are close by.

2. **Reward yourself when you're done.** Let's say you want to devote the next hour and a quarter to a particularly difficult element of the course that's been eluding you. Instead of lashing yourself to the mast and braving the elements, promise yourself, say, a listen to a recently purchased CD upon completion of the task. When you start to droop a half-hour into your task, focus on this reward. You'll boost your morale and make better progress!

3. **Be disciplined—but flexible—and learn to adjust as you go along.** Don't beat yourself up for starting your reading at 10:15 when you had it slotted to begin at 10:10. It's a waste of energy, and you can't afford it. Use time overruns to help you make more realistic forecasts next time.

4. Don't disengage immediately when presented with an unignorable distraction. Before you answer the phone, process the pressing question your roommate is shouting at you or make breakfast for the child who got up a little earlier than you thought she would, take a few seconds to be sure you've reached a logical stopping point in your study work. You'll spend less time spinning your wheels when you come back to the work. Whenever possible, jot down a brief note that will remind you of where you left off.

5. Don't skip around; first things first. Finish one task before you move on to the next one. Moving from topic to topic takes mental energy. Make the shift only after you've completed what you needed to. And remember the planning principle: Get the toughest, highest-priority items on the list out of the way first!

6. If something in your personal study routine doesn't work for you, toss it and try something new. For some people, study groups are a great idea. For others, they're a pain in the neck. For some people, absolute quiet is an essential while studying. For others, Pearl Jam on the headphones is a great way to get the motor running. Experiment until you find what makes you most productive and then stick with it.

7. Monitor your progress toward important goals. Schedules and hour-by-hour strategies are nice, but give yourself the freedom to try a new approach when a planning strategy has had a day or two to deliver the goods and hasn't done so for you.

8. Write everything down. There's a Chinese saying that goes something like this: "The faintest pencil mark is superior to the clearest memory." If you've got a good idea, commit it to paper. If you finish something, cross it off the list—and save yourself the aggravation of finding you've duplicated your efforts later on down the line.

9. Bear in mind the complexity of the assignment when you allocate time slots. Aggressive scheduling is one thing, parting the Red Sea is another. If you try to cram too much work into too little time, you'll reduce your personal effectiveness and increase your frustration level. That makes whatever you have to do next less likely to turn out well. Make realistic time estimates, and adjust them as necessary.

10. Take care of the equipment. Your mind and body are marvelous assets—don't misuse them. Get the sleep you need. Get the nutrition you need.

Month	Mon	Tue	Wed	Thu	Fri	Sat	Sun
← Feb	18	19	20	21	22	23	24
Feb →	25	26	27 Conference 4-5	28	1	2	3
← March	4	5	6	7	8 Afternoon: A.A.P. meeting	9	10
March	11 Sociology Presentation	12	13 Math: Ch. 1-3	14	15	16	17 Trip Home
March →	18	19	20 Math: Ch 4	21	22	23	24

Priority Rating	Scheduled?	Priority Tasks This Week Week of 3/28 through 4/3
		Sociology Paper
H		- Library Search
M		- Outline
L		- Rough Draft
		Math Assignments
H		- Ch. 4
M		- Ch. 5
M		- Study for test

Daily Schedule date: 3/30

Assignments Due	Schedule	
Bio. Lab work.	5	
Math, Ch. 4	6	
	7	
	8	
	9	Biology
To Do/Errands	10	Sociology
Call Erin - 871-4031	11	↓↓
Books to library	12	Lunch w/ Kim
☐ Bank	1	read:
☐ Groceries	2	Ch. 5 (Soc.)
Drop by Jim's	3	Math class
	4	TRAVEL
	5	
Homework	6	Math homework
1) Math Ch. 5 1-9	7	work on paper
2) Sociology paper	8	
(rough draft)	9	
	10	
	11	
	12	

Term Planning Calendar

Fill in due dates for assignments and papers, dates of tests, and important non-academic activities and events

Month	Mon	Tue	Wed	Thu	Fri	Sat	Sun

Priority Rating	Scheduled?	**Priority Tasks This Week** *Week of* ______ *through* ______

Daily Schedule

date:

Assignments Due	Schedule
	5
	6
	7
	8
	9
To Do/Errands	10
	11
	12
	1
	2
	3
	4
	5
Homework	6
	7
	8
	9
	10
	11
	12

Chapter 3

Some essential memory skills: Part 1

Important note: Learning to study is a neglected art, and learning to use one's memory efficiently is one of the most important aspects of that art. The next two chapters contain some of the most important material you will ever come across with regard to memory development. If you've done some memory training in the past, some of this material will be familiar. Nevertheless, *do not skip these chapters;* use them as a tune-up.

Throughout Chapters 3 and 4, the text instructs you to put the book down and take a break. Do so! You may even decide to read the chapters on two consecutive days, so that you have the chance to "sleep on" all the principles covered. Fine, but *do take a break from your reading.* You should not attempt to "cram" all the material that follows. Instead, allow it to settle in and become second nature. If you follow the instructions as written, you'll discover a powerful, simple memory system that will help you in your studies—and in business and personal settings—for the rest of your life.

Pop quiz!

Following you will find a list of facts, roughly equivalent to those you might have to memorize for study purposes. The questions that immediately follow them will test your powers of memorization as they stand right now, before you learn about some of the simple memory-improvement techniques we'll be outlining in this chapter. *Take the test, and read all of the material that appears in this chapter and the next, before you proceed.*

Give yourself 10 minutes to review the material that follows. Then give yourself two minutes to answer the questions associated with them on pages 30 to 31. Mark your answers on a separate sheet of paper. Ready? Go!

- William Shakespeare died in 1616.
- A *Zuccheto* is a small, round skullcap worn by Roman Catholic ecclesiastics.
- The Pythagorean Theorem states that $a^2 + b^2 = c^2$, where a, b and c represent the lengths of the sides of a right triangle.
- William Harvey (1578-1657) demonstrated that blood moves through the body in only one direction, along the veins and arteries.
- In ancient Greek mythology, Zeus was the king of the gods, and the god of the sky and thunder. In Roman mythology, this figure is known as Jupiter.
- The French word for "lawyer" is *avocat.*
- The first American daily newspaper was the *Pennsylvania Evening Post*, founded by Benjamin Towne in 1783.
- Carbon dioxide, or CO_2, is a compound made up of molecules that contain one carbon atom and two oxygen atoms.
- Jean-Paul Marat was an 18th-century French political leader who was one of the most prominent Jacobins, a group of radicals who played an important part in the French Revolution of 1789.
- There are four human blood types: A, B, O and AB.

- President Ulysses S. Grant's opponent in the election of 1872 was newspaper publisher Horace Greeley. Despite the presence of scandal in his administration, Grant soundly defeated Greeley in the November contests. Greeley died after the popular vote, but before the electoral college cast its vote, the first such instance in American history.
- In William Shakespeare's *Othello,* Iago serves as a selfish, dishonest and highly disruptive representative of society; Desdemona, by contrast, shows unfailing love, honesty and trust in all her interactions with others.
- Our moon is about 2,000 miles in diameter; it is approximately 240,000 miles away from us.
- The German artist George Grosz used distortion and caricature to express his loathing of the self-indulgence and hypocrisy he saw in the post-First World War Berlin of his day. Grosz was a leading member of the Dada movement.
- The Korean War began in June 1950.
- Rene Descartes (1596-1650) invented analytical geometry.
- Sir Walter Raleigh, having journeyed to the New World, introduced the tobacco and potato plants to England.
- The evacuation of the last occupying British troops from Iraq took place in October 1947.
- Theodore Roosevelt assumed the presidency of the United States on September 14, 1901, upon the assassination of William McKinley by anarchist Leon Czolgosz.
- The population of Nairobi, Kenya, is estimated by one source to be 1,482,386.

- The world's first atomic bomb was exploded at Alamagordo, New Mexico, on July 16, 1945. The bomb was the result of three years of feverish work on the part of some of the most distinguished scientists in America, who had gathered to take part in the top-secret "Manhattan Project" in 1942.
- In Chinese mythology, Zao-jun is the kitchen god, and his shrine typically occupies a prominent place in that part of a family's dwelling. Once a mortal, he committed suicide as a result of a deception his wife foisted on him, but was granted immortality because of his good qualities. Once a year, he reports to the supreme deity on the doings of the family whose home he inhabits.
- In 1922, total U.S. membership in the Ku Klux Klan was estimated at 5 million. The number of adults in the country at that time was approximately 60 million—which meant that roughly one in every 12 American adults was a member of the fundamentalist racist organization.
- Tom Stoppard's play *Rosencrantz and Guildenstern Are Dead* is a dark parody of Shakespeare's *Hamlet,* heavily influenced by Samuel Beckett's nihilistic *Waiting for Godot.*

Without referring back, answer these questions from memory. Do not check your answers against the text:

1. In what year was Rene Descartes born?
2. What was the name of the newspaper Benjamin Towne began publishing in 1783?
3. In what year did Ulysses S. Grant run for president against Horace Greeley?
4. Who assassinated President McKinley?
5. How far away is the moon from the earth?

6. Where and when was the world's first atomic bomb exploded?
7. Which compound is made up of molecules that contain two oxygen atoms and one carbon atom?

Do not go back to the material you studied.
Answers:

1. 1596.
2. The *Pennsylvania Evening Post.*
3. 1872.
4. Leon Czolgosz.
5. 240,000 miles.
6. July 16, 1945, at Alamagordo, New Mexico.
7. Carbon dioxide (CO_2).

If you got all seven of these correct, congratulations! You probably have an excellent *natural* memory. Unless you have a *trained* memory, though, you should still review the principles in this chapter.

If you missed one or more of the questions, read on. We're going to continue with the next section and learn how to apply some simple memory techniques to the material you just studied. *Do not go back and review the questions.*

Your pathway to a better memory

Obviously, being able to memorize material such as we just reviewed, and being able to do so in a hurry, is a significant advantage when it comes to preparing for tests. It doesn't hurt when you need to master key points from your notes before writing a paper, either.

You *can* improve your memory just about instantly, and this chapter's going to show you exactly how. There are three main methods for memory improvement, and although they may take some time to perfect, they don't take much time at all to learn. And they can deliver results so quickly they'll surprise you.

What follows is a condensed summary of some basic memory techniques that have been helping students, speakers, business people and stage performers for centuries. For a more in-depth review of the subject, take a look at my book, *Improve Your Memory,* available at your local bookstore, or Harry Lorayne's and Jerry Lucas's *The Memory Book,* which you can probably find at your local library. Both of these go into far greater detail than I can here—but the name of the game at this point is speed, right?

Three basic methods for memory improvement

Acronyms
Replacement / Exaggeration
Numerical Sounds

These three methods may have fancy-sounding names, but the ideas behind them are *extremely simple.* No special aptitude, intelligence or training is required to use them and to dramatically increase your efficiency when it comes to studying. We'll look at each of the techniques in detail and you'll see how powerful a few *very straightforward* ideas can be when it comes to memory improvement.

By the way, there is a fourth—and extremely powerful—method, one that combines the basics of all three of the techniques you're about to discover. We'll deal with that strategy, which I call Power Listing, in the next chapter.

If you have a test *now...*

You're about to learn some powerful techniques for improving your memory, and you should know ahead of time that there's a certain amount of self-testing involved in mastering these ideas. This self-testing process won't take you that long, but if you are under *severe* time pressure in preparing for a test—if the test is, say, tomorrow—you will probably want to review all the basic principles covered in this chapter, skip the testing sections, then proceed to Chapter 8 to get some helpful advice on additional ideas you can use to improve your memory instantly.

You'll also want to review the advice on skimming first, and reading for detail later, that appears in Chapter 5.

If you have more than a few days to prepare for your test, however, then you should certainly follow all the advice in the following two chapters, and that includes working with the self-test material.

The three basic methods you're about to learn are essentially the same as those offered by the high-priced "ultra-memory" courses you've probably seen on television commercials late at night. Weren't you a little bit curious about how people could develop those high-powered memory techniques those courses promised? Well, now you don't have to spend $150 to find out.

The three ideas are likely to have greater impact on increasing your personal efficiency when it comes to test preparation than any other part of your study regimen. Don't skip the tests and activities that follow! Review each item closely until you feel comfortable with it, and take breaks at each point you are directed to by the text.

Acronyms

CREEP was the unfortunate name assigned to President Nixon's *Committee to RE-Elect the President.*

The four notes that fall on the treble scale's "open spaces" are *F, A, C* and *E.* Music students are taught to remember the word *FACE* when they first encounter the treble scale.

Radio and television stations often opt for call letters that spell out words or parts of words that relate to the type of programming they offer. In New York, there's a sports-oriented radio station called WFAN.

If you can take a *real, meaningful word* and assign meanings to each of its initial letters, you can often master complex material quickly. Many people make the mistake of developing nonsense acronyms—like QIJA or FEWOP—and then wonder why they can't recall the word when test time roles around! You're after emotion-laden words like MIDAS or BETRAY. If you can associate words like *those* with the key concepts you're studying, you'll be in a much better position. The same principle can be applied to sentences such as "Every Good Boy Does Fine," although I prefer to take the time to develop a good solid acronym that relates directly to whatever it is you're studying.

Developing good acronyms may seem a little tricky at first, but it really isn't. Read and *closely review* the following examples. (There *will* be a test!)

In William Shakespeare's Othello, Iago serves as a selfish, dishonest and highly disruptive representative of society; Desdemona, by contrast, shows unfailing love, honesty and trust in her interactions with others.

A question to ask about the hero of the play, Othello, as he struggles between these two influences: IS HE DULL? In other words, is he a little slow on the uptake? Has he missed something important? He sure has. He's missed *two* important somethings:

***I*ago:**	***D*esdemona:**
*S*elfish,	*U*nfailingly
*H*ateful	*L*oving
*E*gotist;	*L*ady.

Please review the "IS HE DULL?" acronym several times before proceeding.

◆ ❖ ◆ ❖ ◆ ❖ ◆

There are four human blood types: A, B, O, and AB.

An observation about the four blood types: Any Other Blood's Abnormal.

*A*ny *O*ther *B*lood's *AB*-normal.

Note how the order of the second and third elements were reversed in order to make memorization a little easier. In many cases, such as this one, the elements being memorized are more important than the order in which they appear, and a change of order makes no difference. Note, too, that the final entry, "AB-normal," calls a certain amount of attention to itself by offering a slight variation to the expected pattern.

Please review the "Any Other Blood's AB-normal" acronym several times before proceeding.

◆ ❖ ◆ ❖ ◆ ❖ ◆

In ancient Greek mythology, Zeus was the king of the gods, and the god of the sky and thunder. In Roman mythology, this figure is known as Jupiter.

Zeus' two favorite types of music? JAZZ AND REGGAE! Picture him with a chic black beret instead of a crown and his great beard braided into massive dreadlocks.

*J*upiter
*A*nd
*Z*eus—
*Z*apping
*A*ll
*N*earby!
*D*ouble
*R*oman
*E*ntity,
*G*reek
*G*od
*A*ims
*E*xpertly

This acronym provides you with a florid, but nevertheless memorable "headline" that reinforces the following key facts: Jupiter and Zeus are the same entity; they represent Roman and Greek versions, respectively, of the same figure; they have the power to hurl thunderbolts!

Please review your mental image of the beret-clad, dreadlock-bearded Zeus—and the JAZZ AND REGGAE acronym—several times before proceeding.

◆ ❖ ◆ ❖ ◆ ❖ ◆

Sir Walter Raleigh, having journeyed to the New World, introduced the tobacco and potato plants to England.

"Raleigh" sounds like "rally"—think of the PIT CREW that attends to car and driver during a stock car rally. (If it helps you, you can picture Raleigh himself, in full Elizabethan wardrobe, behind the wheel.)

*P*otatoes?
*I*ndeed.
*T*obacco?
*C*ertainly!
*R*aleigh,
*E*ngland's
*W*anderer!

Please review the PIT CREW acronym several times before proceeding.

Can you mentally review the specifics of these passages—Othello, the blood types, Zeus, Sir Walter Raleigh—without consulting the book? Try it now. If not, review the acronyms again, and return to this paragraph.

No problem with the acronyms? *Congratulations!* Developing your own acronyms is a matter of personal preference and just a little practice—and you'll have the chance to get that practice before too long.

For right now, give yourself a reward. Take a *mandatory* break of at least 10 minutes before you proceed. Listen to a favorite song or enjoy a high-energy snack to celebrate your accomplishment! Then, return to master the next technique for memorization.

Replacement/exaggeration

Replacement is simply the process of substituting a boring word or phrase with a more interesting one and using the second word to remind you of the first. If you need to remember the French word for lawyer, "avocat" (pronounced AH-vo-CAH), you might replace it with the phrase "avocado."

Exaggeration is the process whereby you connect the two ideas with something outlandish or oversized. Picture, let's say, a nationally known lawyer from a famous criminal trial of recent date. Does anyone come to mind? (If not, I'll assume you've been on Mars for the last few years, and ask you to pick a specific lawyer you know or a lawyer from a favorite crime drama.)

The person you pick must be a specific individual—not an abstract embodiment of lawyers as a group. To use *exaggeration* to fuse the two ideas ("avocado" and "lawyer"), imagine that lawyer making the closing argument to a jury, picking up a foot-tall avocado and smashing it on top of his head. See the green goop trailing down on his suit.

When it comes time to remember the word for "lawyer," you'll recall that absurd image. And you'll remember "avocado." And your "natural" memory will kick in with "avocat."

Replacement—finding the interesting word or phrase that sounds enough like the boring one to make your "natural" memory kick in—is a pretty basic technique, and there's not much to it. In the following examples, you'll see more instances of replacement in action.

Exaggeration, on the other hand, can take many forms and merits a little fuller discussion here. (In most cases, when people can't get memory systems to deliver results for them, it's because they haven't mastered the technique of exaggeration.) Take a look at this sentence:

> *"Some people don't like to eat worms—but I certainly do!"*

If I told you that you had to memorize that sentence, word for word and recall it for an exam, would you be able to do that? Of course you would.

What exactly makes that sentence memorable? For one thing, it summons up a vivid, unforgettable image (eating worms). For another, that image is a bit nauseating. Finally, it reverses your expectations about the situation and creates an unexpected connection. (Who on earth would brag about *liking* to eat worms?) All three of those factors can be put to work in your efforts to turn your study material into *specific images* you can manipulate—and recall—easily.

A *vivid, exaggerated, unforgettable image* is one that has direct, immediate visual appeal. A five-inch-long, dangling, wriggling worm on the end of a fork is a vivid image. However, a *sign* that says "WORMS FOR SALE" is not—it's vague, undramatic, not exaggerated and not visually oriented. So you're going to construct pictures that are based in *one vivid, exaggerated picture at a time.*

An image with *exaggerated gut-level associations* is one that plays on our natural human tendency to remember that which is striking on a visceral level. Once you've pictured yourself moving a *forkful* of those huge, wriggling worms toward your open mouth, then closing your mouth around the fork and actually chewing the worms, you've conjured up a situation you're not soon likely to forget.

On the other hand, if you picture yourself pondering a can of worms on a supermarket shelf, you probably *will* forget that. The second image is not rooted in sensory reactions, danger and/or violence or romance. And those are signals human beings tend to pay attention to.

An image that *reverses our expectations in an exaggerated way* is one that sends the mind reeling. "Some people don't like to eat worms..." (Our mind wonders: "*Some* people?") "...but I certainly do!" (Your mind concludes: "I *do*? Call the psychiatrist!") When things go as we expect them to, we generally pay no notice. It's no big deal if some people don't like to eat *spaghetti,* but I do. Replace the pasta with the little crawly fellas and the mind sits up and takes notice.

Bearing these three principles in mind, let's see how they can be used to help us remember specific study facts.

A Zuccheto is a small, round skullcap worn by Roman Catholic ecclesiastics.

Zuccheto (sounds like "zoo cat ow"): Imagine that dozens of these tiny round caps have been nailed onto your head by a priest. In order to pry them loose, you have to put your head inside a *zoo,* where a huge *cat* tears the caps off one by one with massive paws and tosses them back outside the cage at you. (Picture an enlarged version of a cat you're familiar with, preferably your own.) It smarts...a little...as the cat takes the caps off! You say "*ow*!"—and the cat stops.

The Pythagorean Theorem states that $a^2 + b^2 = c^2$, *where a, b, and c represent the lengths of the sides of a right triangle.*

Look at $a^2 + b^2 = c^2$ (sounds like "ape, square, bee, square, sea, square"). Picture this. You are trying to leave a print of your paintsoaked right hand (*right triangle)* on the back of...King Kong! The monster (*ape*) is playing hopscotch (*square*) by stomping through your city's streets, obliterating buildings. On one of the spots where Kong stomps is a *square bee*hive; a massive bee uses its stinger to pick up the yellow plastic borders of the gargantuan hopscotch game (*square)* and tosses it into the *sea* with a gigantic splash. You can see the huge *squares* floating on the ocean for miles as they stretch toward the horizon.

Don't think of the sequence above as a *story*—think of it as a series of vivid images stacked together. Stories tend to get lost or reinvented; single images stapled together, one after another, will stay with you.

- *right* palmprint you're trying to place on back of *ape*
- *ape* playing hopscotch on *squares* laid out over city
- *square bee*hive
- *bee* carrying plastic hopscotch outline (*squares*) in its stinger
- yellow plastic *squares* being tossed into *sea* and making huge splash
- *sea* supporting *squares* as they stretch into horizon

I call this type of sequence a *memory chain.* It connects two or more mental images in a kind of latticework:

AB

(right/ape)

BC

(ape/square)

CD

(square/bee) ...and so on.

The memory chain's first element should be the strong *central idea* you will think of *first,* before trying to recall the supplementary information.

In this case, you would *not* want to memorize the letters of the formula first, and then supply the name or purpose of the formula—something related to right triangles, which would jog your "natural" memory about the Pythagorean Theorem—at the end of the chain! *Put the big idea up front,* and proceed to connect the supporting bits of information together one at a time.

By the same token, memorizing the formula without attaching it to *anything* won't do you much good. When it comes time to recall the information for the test, you may waste time trying to think of the first element of the formula, rather than the purpose to which it will be put!

A few more brief notes on the way we have constructed this series of images are probably in order: First of all, notice that we did *not* try to picture a "giant letter A" or a "huge C" in memorizing the formula. These sorts of mnemonics are simply too abstract to "stick." Use substitute words instead, not enlarged letters or numbers.

Secondly, because the formula we're trying to remember is fairly simple, your "natural" memory will probably supply some key information. In a more elaborate formula, you would probably want to incorporate a mnemonic that helps you to retain the "equals" sign. I use a set of parallel bars—the kind gymnasts work out on—as my symbol.

Finally, as with any memory aid, you must *review* the material after having assembled the pictures in your mind the first time, preferably after you've spent a few moments away from them, concentrating on something else.

Important note: Many people, when it's time to implement the basics of image-related memory techniques, rely too strongly on the idea of one strange image simply "turning into" another one. This is usually not a good memory technique for connecting two ideas. You should try to incorporate some unexpected, or even violent, connection between the two ideas in question, rather than simply allowing one to fade into another. The fadeouts themselves will begin to fade together after a while!

The system I'm describing, which may seem elaborate at first, works on two levels and is worth pursuing because of that double action. When it comes time to re-examine the images, your mind will work through each one and play the entire sequence to your "mind's eye." At the same time, *the simple act of going through the process of associating images with each element of the idea,* a process that takes only seconds per image, will have strengthened your familiarity with the initial concept—and will probably result in your simply recalling the formula immediately from your "natural" memory!

In Chinese mythology, Zao-jun is the kitchen god, and his shrine typically occupies a prominent place in that part of a family's dwelling. Once a mortal, he committed suicide as a result of a deception his wife foisted on him, but was granted immortality because of his good qualities. Once a year, he reports to the supreme deity on the doings of the family whose home he inhabits.

Zao-jun (sounds like "sew June"): Imagine that you are in *your* kitchen or a kitchen you remember from your childhood. (This will remind you of the *kitchen* god.) You are trying to *sew* a small plaster statue to the stove and it's not going well—the needle keeps breaking. *June* Lockhart—the mother from the old *Lassie* series—takes over, and starts sewing *you* to her apron! (If there's another idea that is richer in association for you than Ms. Lockhart—a friend you know by the name of June, for instance—feel free to use that idea.)

If you wanted to strengthen the other elements of the passage, incorporate more images into a longer string.

Take a moment now to review the images we've tied to each of these four ideas: *zuccheto, avocat,* right triangle, kitchen god.

Can you recall all the key principles, simply by means of reviewing those absurd images? If not, review all the associations once again, then try to recall them without looking at the book. If so, congratulations! You've mastered the second memorization method, replacement/exaggeration. Take a *mandatory* break of at least 10 minutes before you proceed to the next section of the book.

Welcome back! Assuming you are rested and ready to roll, you're about to learn about one of the most powerful study techniques ever to come down the pike. Stick with it and follow *all the instructions exactly as written.* I promise you, you won't regret it!

Numerical sounds (sounds—and digits?)

Seems kind of silly, doesn't it? We associate the "ssssss" sound with the letter "S"—but what sound do we associate with, say, the digit zero?

Unlikely as it may seem at first, there is a 10-digit phonetic "alphabet" tied to each of the numbers in our counting system. This alphabet makes it easy to remember even long-number sequences like this one:

03995121571143091041251

Within the phonetic number alphabet you're about to learn to put to your advantage, the digit zero *does* have a sound—it makes a "ssssss" sound, just like the letter "S." It also makes the related "zzzzzz" sound of the letter "Z."

There are *no vowels* within this number system—or rather, there are whatever vowels you want to incorporate. There's no sound associated with the letters "H," "W" or "Y," either, so you can stick them in wherever you want when it's time to form a word.

Even if you're not the greatest speller, this system can work wonders for you. It is based *completely on the sound of a word in question.* Silent letters mean absolutely nothing. Letters that sound like other are treated as though they are those letters. How the word *sounds* dictates everything. As a result, the single digit "0," which makes the same sounds as "S" and "Z," can mean a lot of different things—each of which is a good deal more interesting than some abstract number. For instance...

If you needed to remember the digit "0," you could picture it as your own EYES. The word EYES has only one consonant sound—S—and can mean only one number: zero!

You could also have pictured the "0" as a *house* ("H" is ignored, just like a vowel), or some *ice,* or as an *Ace* from a pack of cards. All of these words can mean *only "0."*

What about the other digits? Well, the number "1" has a sound, too. If you were to make one tiny dot on the blank sheet, how many marks would there be on the piece of paper? One, of course. One dot for one point on the sheet. And the word *dot* contains the two consonant sounds associated with the number "1": "D" and "T."

If you needed to remember the digit "1," you could picture it as your TOE. The word TOE has only one consonant sound—T—and can mean one and only one number: "1"!

You could also have pictured the digit one as a *head,* or as some *dough,* or as a *tie.* All of these words can mean *only* the number "1."

How about the number "2"? When I think of the number "2," I think of the story of Noah's ark—it was his job to collect two of each type of animal and load them all onto the boat! "N" is for "Noah"—and "N" is for "2," too!

If you needed to remember the digit "2," you could picture it as your KNEE. The word KNEE has only one consonant sound—N—and can mean only one number: "2"!

You could also have pictured the digit "2" as a *Noah* himself, or as a *hen* or as some *honey*. All of these words can mean *only* the number "2."

STOP! Take a moment now to review the sounds associated with the digits "0," "1" and "2." Write them down on a sheet of paper. Write down why each digit has its particular sound. Then return to the book and keep reading.

Have you taken the time to write down, on a separate sheet of paper, the sounds associated with the first three digits? Have you written down *why* each digit sounds the way it does? If you haven't, please take the time to do so now! Much of what follows in this book will not make sense to you if you are not familiar with the phonetic digit system. Write the numbers and the sounds down!

The number "3" makes a sound, too—the "M" sound. The fact that this numeral sort of *looks* like an "M" if you tip it on its side reminds us that the digit "3" makes the "M" sound.

3 m

If you needed to remember the digit "3," you could picture it as your HOME—in other words, the front door of the place where you live. The word HOME has only one relevant consonant sound—M—and can mean only one number: "3"!

You could also have pictured the "3" as a *ham,* or as someone you know whose name is *Emma,* or as a *yam*. All of these words can mean *only* the number "3."

The sound for the number "4" is the "R" sound. The fact that this number *ends* in the "R" sound is the reason these two go together.

If you needed to remember the digit "4," you could picture it as your own EAR. The word EAR has only one consonant sound—R—and can mean only one number: "4"!

You could also have pictured the digit "4" as an *oar,* or as some *hair,* or as an *Oreo*. All of these words can mean *only* the number "4."

The number "5" makes the "L" sound. You may remember the main character from the animated film *An American Tail.* The little mouse's name was Feivel (five-L), which is a good way to remember the sound associated with the number "5."

If you needed to remember the digit "5," you could picture it as your own HEEL. The word HEEL has one relevant consonant sound—L—and can mean only one number: "5"!

You could also have pictured the digit "5" as a *lei,* or as some *ale,* or as an *eel*. All of these words can mean *only* the number "5."

There are a number of sounds associated with the number "6"—but don't worry, they're all easy to recognize. The "J" sound, the "SH" sound, the soft "G" sound and the "CH" sound, are all linked to this number. (If you pronounce all the sounds slowly, you'll realize that all are made with essentially the same positioning of your mouth and tongue.) If you compare a handwritten "6" and a handwritten "J," you'll see that they are nearly mirror images.

6 J

If you needed to remember the digit "6," you could picture it as your own JAW. The word JAW has one relevant consonant sound—J—and can mean only one number: "6"!

You could also have pictured the digit "6" as a *shoe,* or as a *hatch,* or as a *hitch*. All of these words can mean *only* the number "6."

STOP! Take a moment now to review the sounds associated with the digits "3," "4," "5" and "6." Write them down on a sheet of paper. Write down why each digit has its particular sound. When you have done this, return to the book and keep reading.

Have you taken the time to write down, on a separate sheet of paper, the sounds associated with the numbers "3" through "6"? Have you written down *why* each digit sounds the way it does? If you haven't, please take the time to do so now! Much of what follows in this book will not make sense to you if you are not familiar with the phonetic digit system. Write the numbers and the sounds down!

The sounds associated with the number "7" are the "K," hard "C" and hard "G" sounds. (If you pronounce all the sounds slowly, you'll realize that all are made with essentially the same positioning of your mouth and tongue.) Seven is a lucky number—the last sound in the word "luck" is the "K" sound.

If you needed to remember the digit "7," you could picture it as your own KEY—whatever key you use most often, whether that's a house key, apartment key or car key. The word KEY has only one relevant consonant sound—K—and can mean only one number: "7"!

You could also have pictured the digit "7" as a *cow,* or as a *hook,* or as a *hog*. All of these words can mean *only* the number "7."

The sounds associated with the number "8" are the "V," "F" and "PH" sounds. (If you pronounce all the sounds slowly, you'll realize that all are made with essentially the same positioning of your mouth and tongue.) If you make a trip to the local supermarket and ask for the most popular brand of vegetable juice, the manager will probably steer you toward the shelf that has the V-8 juice on display. This familiar product is a good way to remember that the number "8" makes the sounds in the "V" family.

If you needed to remember the digit "8," you could picture it as the biblical character EVE—whatever she represents to you. The word EVE has only one consonant sound—V—and can mean one and only one number: "8"!

You could also have pictured the digit eight as a *hive,* or as some *ivy,* or as a *foe.* All of these words can mean *only* the number "8."

The sounds associated with the number "9" are the "B" and "P" sounds. (If you pronounce both of these sounds slowly, you'll realize that all are made with essentially the same positioning of your mouth.) There are nine players on the field at a time for a *baseball* team, and *baseball* starts with the letter "B."

If you needed to remember the digit "9," you could picture it as your own HIP. The word HIP has one relevant consonant sound—P—and can mean only one number: "9"!

You could also have pictured the digit "9" as a *bee,* or as a *pie,* or as a *hoop.* All of these words can mean *only* the number "9."

STOP! Take a moment now to review the sounds associated with the digits "7," "8" and "9." Write them down on a sheet of paper. Write down why each digit has its particular sound. When you have done this, return to the book and keep reading.

Have you taken the time to write down, on a separate sheet of paper, the sounds associated with the numbers "7" through "9"? Have you written down *why* each digit sounds the way it does? If you haven't, please take the time to do so now! Much of what follows in this book will not make sense to you if you are not familiar with the phonetic digit system. Write the numbers and the sounds down!

Here's a short test—use it to gauge how familiar you are with the principles you've just learned. Trust me on one important point: Although the alphabet may seem a little cumbersome at first, it becomes second nature *very* quickly...and it will, as we will see shortly, pay very impressive dividends for you when it comes to memorizing numbers and number-related materials.

On a piece of paper, and without looking back at the previous pages, answer the following questions:

1. What number does the word JAW translate to?
2. Name a sound that the number "8" makes.
3. What number is associated with the "S" sound?
4. What number does the word HEEL translate to?
5. What number does the word HIP translate to?
6. Name a sound that the number "3" makes.
7. What number is associated with the "T" sound?
8. What number does the word KNEE translate to?
9. Name a sound that the number "4" makes.
10. What number does the word KEY translate to?

All done? Please check your answers below.

If you scored eight or fewer correct, please go back and review the material until you can name all 10 sounds when a friend calls digits out to you at random.

If you scored nine correct, please go back and review the single digit/sound combination that gave you trouble.

If you scored all 10 correct—*congratulations!* The information you now possess is powerful enough to allow you to instantly memorize a *23-digit number!*

Answers:

1. "6"
2. "F," "V" or "Ph"
3. "0"
4. "5"
5. "9"
6. "M"
7. "1"
8. "2"
9. "R"
10. "7"

Feeling skeptical? Don't. Do you remember that imposing string of numbers we saw a little earlier in this chapter?

03995121571143091041251

Don't beat your head against the wall and try to memorize it the way you ordinarily would. ("Zero three...zero three nine...zero three nine nine...") Instead, take a look at this sentence:

> *"Some people don't like to eat worms—but I certainly do!"*

Sound familiar? We saw it earlier in the book, remember? Well, if you can repeat that sentence to yourself, you can recite that impossible-looking 23-digit number that once seemed out of your reach. The long string of numbers is simply a "translation" of that ridiculous sentence!

> *"Some (03) people (995) don't (121) like (57) to (1) eat (1) worms (430)—but (91) I (no numbers, since there are no consonants in the word 'I') certainly (04125) do (1)!"*

Take a few moments now to reward yourself for the memorization ability you've developed so quickly! Put the book down for at least 10 minutes—even overnight—and be sure to give yourself an appropriate reward of some kind for mastering this high-powered learning technology. When you're relaxed, rested and ready to get back to work, return to the book.

Chapter 4

Some essential memory skills: Part 2

You have now seen how a single impossible-to-forget sentence can translate into an impossible-to-forget 23-digit number—something you probably would never have thought yourself capable of memorizing before you picked up this book. Now you're going to learn how to use the process in the opposite direction—by taking the numbers you need to memorize, turning them into words and ideas you can remember and incorporating unusual images that will stick in your mind just as readily as this sentence did:

"Some people don't like to eat worms—but I certainly do!"

The digital alphabet can make hard-to-memorize "abstract" numbers you face instantly memorable. (In the following examples, we'll be memorizing *only* the dates by associating them with the most important single idea of the passage. You can also use the Acronym and Replacement/Exaggeration methods to develop more elaborate memory connections, and to master nonnumerical material as well.)

William Shakespeare died in 1616.

Picture yourself strapping William Shakespeare into an electric chair (*William Shakespeare died...*). As you do so, he begs you to refrain from touching his body—and you scream, "*T*ou*ch*y, *t*ou*ch*y!" (*...in 1616*) before you pull the lever!

William Harvey (1578-1657) demonstrated that blood moves through the body in only one direction, along the veins and arteries.

What do you think of when you hear the name "Harvey"? You might think of the movie that tells the story of a man who has an imaginary rabbit friend by that name. Or you might think of the drink, the Harvey Wallbanger. If either of those connections came to mind, they would be great choices as the first part of a ridiculous image built around the two dates you've been given to memorize.

Another choice, assuming that none of those connections made sense for you, might be the image of a *heart*—a fortunate substitution, considering the nature of the man's work, and one that will help to remind you of the first syllable of his name. For the sake of argument, let's use that one. (But remember—the images you select must work for *you* first and foremost! Find an image that carries strong associations in your own mind.)

On an operating table, a patient's *heart* (William *Harvey*) pumps out, instead of blood, a stream of *hot, oily coffee* (1578). You try to stop the flow with a *dish,* but this breaks instantly, so you pick up a *log* and insert it in the patient's chest, which stops the flow. (*Dish, log* = 1657.) A little disgusting, perhaps, but a series of images not soon forgotten.

The Korean War began in June 1950.

It's a pretty safe bet that you'll remember that the Korean War took place in the 20th century, right? I like to make memorizing dates easier by eliminating the first two digits of all years that begin with the number 19. Let's associate an image from the Korean War—say, the character

Hawkeye, from the television show *M*A*S*H*—with the numbers "6" (for June) and "50" (for 1950), being careful to separate them. You might imagine Hawkeye eating his own *shoe,* then being caught in a gigantic *lasso* that you throw about his midsection until he coughs up the evidence. See the huge circle of rope twisting around his head, then see it squeezing him tighter as you pull on it.

The evacuation of the last occupying British troops from Iraq took place in October 1947.

For Iraq, you might picture Saddam Hussein. For the occupying British troops, you might picture Queen Elizabeth. The Queen is standing on top of the dictator, but he bites her repeatedly on all of her *toes* ("10," for October), prompting her to run away and place a tattered *rag* ("47," for 1947) on her bleeding extremities.

In 1922, total U.S. membership in the Ku Klux Klan was estimated at 5 million. The number of adults in the country at that time was approximately 60 million—which meant that roughly one in every 12 American adults was a member of the fundamentalist racist organization.

A couple of important pieces of information here: Let's first take on the fact that Klan membership in 1922 was 5 million. Picture a white-robed Klansman kicking a *nun* ("22," for 1922) with the back of his *heel.* Not the most pleasant image, but not totally inappropriate to the topic, either, and certainly not difficult to forget.

Now let's look at the approximate population of adults at that time. We'll be forming a basic "memory chain." Picture a *nun* ("22" again, for 1922) arriving at your door and asking you questions from a clipboard for the U.S. census. You have no time for her, so you shove a massive piece of *cheese* ("60," for 60 million) into her mouth, which she seems to understand, because she walks away.

◆ ❖ ◆ ❖ ◆ ❖ ◆

The population of Nairobi, Kenya, is estimated by one source to be 1,482,386.

For "Nairobi" picture a *knight* in your own bath*robe*. He's causing a huge commotion by galloping his horse through a *drive-in movie show* (1,482,386), and he's irritating the patrons by getting in the way of the images on the screen.

◆ ❖ ◆ ❖ ◆ ❖ ◆

Stop! Take a moment now to review all the numerical associations you've just made. When you feel confident with each of them, take a break of at least 10 minutes. Then review *all three* categories of the mnemonic work you've done. Look once again at all the acronyms, replacements and exaggerations and numerical associations you just mastered. The process should take no longer than five minutes or so. Do this right now.

This step is an essential part of the memorization/study process. When it comes time to prepare for your exams, don't skip this step! Take a few moments and review the associations you develop for your *real-life* study material.

An amazing thing happens when you use these systems: *The effort you expend in applying the systems helps your "natural" memory do a better job.* Often, the merest hint of the mnemonic technique you used is all that's necessary to help you recall the information in full.

Now it's time to surprise yourself. Please take the short test on the next page. Write your answers on a separate sheet of paper.

Memory Test

Without referring to the previous pages, please mark your answers on a separate piece of paper.

1. In Shakespeare's play *Othello,* what are the most notable attributes that Desdemona and Iago, respectively, possess? ("Is he dull?")
2. What is the population of Nairobi, Kenya? (Where was the *knight* who was wearing your *robe?)*
3. What is a *Zuccheto?* (What was the *zoo cat* doing that made you say "*ow*"?)
4. What is Zeus's other name? (What kind of music did he like?)
5. When did William Shakespeare die? (What did you say as you were strapping him in?)
6. What is the formula that can help you determine the lengths of the sides of a right triangle? (Where were you trying to put your *right* palmprint?)
7. What is the French word for "lawyer"? (What vegetable did the lawyer use during his closing argument?)

So much for the hints! Now you're on your own....

8. What are the four primary human blood types?
9. In what year was William Harvey born?
10. When did the Korean War begin?
11. Name two plants from the New World that Sir Walter Raleigh introduced to England.
12. What's the name of the Chinese kitchen god?

13. How many Americans belonged to the Ku Klux Klan in 1922?
14. When did occupying British troops withdraw from Iraq?

When you've finished, please turn the book upside down and check the answer key at the bottom of this page.

If you missed one or more of these questions, please go back and strengthen the particular associations that did not hold for you. If necessary, make the pictures more vivid. Then take the test again, answering *all* the questions, until you can provide correct answers for *all* the elements of the test. (Although it may seem repetitive, this approach will help you strengthen your basic association skills.)

If you've answered all of these questions correctly—*congratulations!* You've developed a test-ready memory, the kind that will be of invaluable service to you as you prepare for the study work you face.

To close this chapter, I'd like to ask you to develop your *own* associations with another set of sample test materials, and leave the testing up to you. After each piece of information, I've included a *suggested* plan of attack for memorizing particular aspects of the material. The best memory strategy, however, is the one that works for you.

Ready? Go!

Answers:

1. Iago is a selfish egotist; Desdemona displays unfailing love for others. 2. 1,482,386. 3. A circular skullcap worn by Roman Catholic ecclesiastics. 4. Jupiter. 5. 1616. 6. $a^2 + b^2 = c^2$. *7. Avocat. 8. A, B, O and AB. (Any order in which you provided these four is acceptable.) 9. 1578. 10. June of 1950. 11. Potatoes and tobacco. 12. Zao-jun. 13. Five million. 14. October of 1947.*

Another Memory Test

- In the early 1930s, kinetic artist Alexander Calder constructed modern art's first mobile.

  (I'd stick with replacement words to represent a person's last name, and skip the first name—unless there are multiple instances of that name. Usually, your "natural" memory will kick in with the first name—or you may get by with simply using the last name. However, this approach won't work for you in every case, and you may feel more comfortable developing images for first and last names.)

- The atomic number for the element silver is 107.868. The symbol for this element is *Ag*.

  (To separate the "107" part from the "868" part, use two separate images. Candidates for the "107" number: tusk, disk or white sack; candidates for the "868" number: half a shave, fudge fee or fetch eve. Recall it in the correct sequence! As for memorizing the symbol, you'll want to find a word that features AG in the first syllable, one that is rich in meaning for you.)

- George Washington Carver, who was the son of slaves, developed hundreds of industrial uses for southern crops like sweet potatoes and peanuts.

  (A simple memory chain would do the trick here. The name Carver practically memorizes itself; the first half of your image should make use of the idea of someone carving something.)

- Our sun is approximately 4.5 billion years old.

  (You may want to develop a personal approach to dealing with "billions and billions" of things. I prefer to simply incorporate a dollar bill into the picture, which is my shorthand for "billion.")

- The Roman conquest of Gaul (present-day France) took place between 57 and 50 B.C.

  (Besides the numbers, for which you should now start developing words and phrases on your own, be sure you connect the possibly unfamiliar word "Gaul" with the idea of "France," which I usually represent with a loaf of French bread.)

- The principal languages of Belgium are Dutch and French.

  (As you apply your personal mnemonic systems to your study material, you'll become more familiar with "shorthand" images that represent specific, common ideas. Objects associated with particular countries are one type of "shorthand": My images for Holland and France are a wooden shoe and a loaf of French bread, respectively.)

- The president installed in Panama after the 1989 ouster of Manuel Noriega was Guillermo Endara.

  (You may—or may not—decide to adopt my system of eliminating the first two digits for years occurring in the 20th century. When it comes to memorizing the foreign names, I recommend using replacement words when you do not already have strong associations with the person in question. It's possible that you have such an association with Noriega; for Endara, you will probably decide to develop replacement-word images for his name.)

- The government that led Germany during the period between the end of World War I and Adolf Hitler's assumption of political power in 1933 was known as the Weimar Republic.

  (Weimar is pronounced "vie mar." Be sure you incorporate the appropriate pronunciation in your image-making. Oral exams count, too!)

- The Irish potato famine of the 1840s, caused by successive potato crop failures, led to starvation for many. About 1 million Irish citizens immigrated to the United States during this period.

  (Several distinct bits of information here lead me to the conclusion that a memory chain—several connected images, beginning from a strong central concept—would be the way to go. As with the figure for membership in the Ku Klux Klan in 1922, a single digit—in this case, "1"—is probably sufficient as a means of memorizing "1 million." My own system has incorporated this technique often enough that I easily convert the single digit into the "X million" format, which makes it another type of mental shorthand. The context usually leaves no doubt as to whether, for instance, one Irish citizen, or one million, is involved!)

- Islam is a monotheistic religion that originated in Arabia through the Prophet Muhammad. Muhammad was born in Mecca in 570 A.D.

  ("Monotheistic" is a 25-cent word that means simply "worshipping a single God." Here, the majority of the work to be done lies in breaking down intimidating or overwrought writing into its simplest forms. Don't try to memorize passages you don't understand. Look up what you need. An image of a single God might take many forms; use the one that is most memorable for you.)

- George Clinton served as vice-president of the United States under Thomas Jefferson.

  (This one is a good candidate for an acronym. In a memory chain, you might be tempted to replace Vice-President George Clinton with President Bill Clinton when recalling the material. By developing an

acronym from a unique sentence that is both meaningful and memorable to you, you'll get cues that will point you toward the correct first and last names. This short passage offers an example of an exception to my general rule about dealing with last names. See the note on the Calder passage earlier.)

- The lymphatic system consists primarily of lymph vessels, which carry the fluid lymph around the human body—and through the lymph nodes and certain glands. Lymph, which resembles blood without the red cells, contains many white cells the body uses to fight infection.

  (When dealing with technical material, be sure that you associate key ideas—such as the ability of lymph to fight infection—with your replacement words. Don't memorize the words in the abstract, with nothing connecting them to a concept you understand.)

- Argentina seized the British-controlled Falkland Islands in 1982, but Britain launched heavy military assaults and resumed control of the islands.

  (In a deceptively simple-looking passage, it's easy to overlook key elements. I was tempted to memorize simply "Falklands" and "1982"—but then I realized that I had no idea of the identity of the country with which Britain had gone to war! I knew it was in South America—was it Chile? Brazil? Argentina? Be sure you incorporate all the necessary elements into your memory chain.)

- The earliest known compass was used in China around 1100 A.D.

  (Developing images for numbers with repeating sets of digits may take a little more work, but you'll get

used to these figures after a while. Candidates for this one include Dad's house, tot Sis or toad sauce. That last one sounds delicious, doesn't it? Important note: Relying on plurals to develop words with lots of "S" sounds can be problematic. I don't like images like dead aces for the number above, because my mind doesn't usually hold on to the idea of more than one ace when it comes time to recall the material.)

- Light travels through a vacuum at a rate of approximately 186,000 miles per second.

  (Another tricky multiple "S" problem; I recommend taking the time to develop a phrase that accommodates all the digits, like "Dave chews a see-saw," for this one all the way up to the number 999,999. As I've noted earlier, my approach is to use context for single digits that represent numbers in the millions, and to incorporate a shorthand symbol—a dollar bill—for single digits that represent numbers in the billions.)

- The battle of Waterloo, which took place in Belgium in 1815, marked Napoleon's defeat at the hands of the British.

  (Make stereotypes work for you! When it comes to major historical figures like Napoleon, you may have an image of a short, dark-haired fellow with one hand thrust into his coatfront in your mind. Use that image as a starting point, and then make sure your character does something outlandlishly exaggerated for the first image—like finding a dripping toilet—water / loo—in his coat!)

In conclusion

You've had enough book testing, right? Use your own preferred method for testing the associations you've just made to the simulated study material. My suggestion would be to write each topic down on a piece of paper while looking at the book, then check all your images, acronyms and connections after putting the book away, by looking only at the topic headings you wrote down. Write down each of the specific items you memorized. (This is an excellent way to strengthen associations, as is reading material out loud.) *The more you practice, the better your trained memory will become.*

In the next chapter, you'll learn about the specific steps you should take when preparing for an exam that is 10 to 15 days away. You'll find out how to map your strategy and allocate your time intelligently, how to outline study materials effectively and how to use the three memory techniques we've outlined in this chapter as part of a single, extremely effective memorization method I call *Power Listing*. (Whether or not you have 10 to 15 days to plan your exam, you should probably review the Power Listing material closely before you proceed to other parts of the book.)

Before you move on, take a well-deserved break from your memory work. Put on a favorite song and kick back for a few minutes. You've worked hard to master the techniques in this chapter—and you've done just that! Enjoy yourself before you move on to the next portion of the book. That's an order!

Chapter 5

If you have a test in 10 to 15 days

Plan your time before you start: Follow the advice in Chapter 2—and develop a written battle plan!

Use your Planning Calendar, your weekly Priority Task Sheet and your Daily Schedule to allocate the time available to prepare for the test. Isolate the most important elements of the exam you must prepare for, and give them highest priority.

Whenever possible, schedule your test preparation activities for your own personal "prime time." Keep all appropriate written planning materials in your Study Plan Central book. Monitor your progress toward key goals on a *daily* basis.

Here's a *suggested* breakdown of the major study issues you could choose to focus on, assuming you have 12 days at your disposal. Of course, your own class, work and personal schedules will necessitate that you develop a unique schedule that works for *you,* rather than marching lockstep through this outline.

- **Days 12 to 9:** Review your written materials extensively. (See the section on skimming and reading for detail in this chapter.)
- **Days 8 to 6:** Develop "condensed notes" (later in this chapter) and review your own notes from class.

- **Days 7 to 4:** Work with others in your class, or with friends or family members, on developing strategies and potential responses to the upcoming exam. If you can, track down previous examples of tests from this instructor.
- **Day 3:** Review the test-taking strategies outlined in Chapter 13 of this book.
- **Days 2 and 1:** Develop a Power List covering key materials (you'll find the technique outlined later in this chapter).
- **The morning of the test:** Review your notes...and then practice using your mental Power List as a means of transferring your "condensed notes" to paper *without* consulting your notes. (If you can do this relatively quickly and have the opportunity to take notes during the test, you will probably want to *quickly and accurately* transfer the notes to paper during your exam period.)

Skim first, then read for detail

The most effective way to get the key points from any reading assignment is to *skim* the material first, then head back over it once again to catch key details. If you perform both of these steps with a highlighter or marker in your hand, you can isolate critical pieces of information that you will use later to build your Power List. By the way, *skimming* is different from *scanning.* When you *skim* a written text (or collection of handwritten notes), you:

- Review all headlines and headings closely—perhaps rephrasing the ideas you find there in the form of a question, to be sure you understand the material. (Saying the headings out loud is a good idea, too.)

- Look at all graphics, illustrations and subheadings that may show up.
- Thoroughly read all *introductory* paragraphs. Yes, even though you're scanning, you do need to review the vital "here's-what-this-chapter-is-about" stuff closely. Introductory material often outlines the rest of the text in an accessible, user-friendly way. (For technical subjects: If you are studying math, science or other technically imposing topics, be sure to take the time to work through and understand all relevant formulas, equations, graphs and charts throughout the section you are studying. *Do not* move on to the step outlined next. Technical topics require mastery of the problems and strategies posed before you can progress. Even if you have to backtrack a little, make sure you have a thorough grasp of the specifics of your topic before you move to the next section.)
- Closely read the *first sentence* of each paragraph. This part of the text usually (but not always) contains the main idea.
- Review what you've learned from following the above steps, and develop questions for deeper review of the text. Don't be afraid to *say things out loud*—this is an excellent memory aid and study technique!

Skimming, the steps of which I've just outlined, is an essential study technique. It corresponds to the SQ3R—Survey, Question, Read, Recite, Review—technique you may have learned about in school. *Scanning* is the process of looking for a *specific fact or reference* from your materials. The two ideas are often confused.

Throughout this skimming process, don't be afraid to highlight the key ideas you come across. Some people get skittish when it comes time to use a colored marker to highlight in their books. When we were children, our parents told us never to write in books. Now, as we prepare for tests or develop material for written reports, the books are *ours* to do with as we please. (Don't write in books you don't own—make photocopies and work from those.)

Effective outlining doesn't mean coloring every other sentence of the text in yellow. That's a waste of time. Effective outlining means *tearing the heart out of the material you're reading.* It means bypassing minor details the first time around, and using your highlighter or marker to place a flashing sign next to the most essential, most fundamental ideas. You can also use your highlighter to point up key facts and details you come across during your second read. If you are skimming effectively, however, most highlighting will be done the first time you go over the text.

In other words, you must use your highlighter to establish, and note for later use and study, every important *concept*, *name*, *formula* or *date*.

Skimming practice

Here is a stretch of text that deals with American history. Follow the skim-first-and-review-for-detail-later advice as you read through it. *Make marks in this book!* Use your highlighter to emphasize the key ideas.

The troubled Grant Administration: five scandals

Five major scandals tainted the administration of President Ulysses S. Grant. Although the hero of Vicksburg was the first chief executive to encounter serious, credible charges of substantial wrongdoing within his presidency, he himself was never convincingly associated with any direct involvement in criminal acts. The first of the five unsavory incidents came in 1869, the first year of the Civil War hero's presidency, and was known as Black Friday.

Black Friday

Speculators James Fisk and Jay Gould aimed to corner the gold market. They enlisted the assistance of the President's brother-in-law in an attempt to gain influence within the White House as it established the nation's financial policies, and hoped to prevent the government from "dumping" its gold onto the market, a step that would make their scheme impossible to carry out.

The two also entertained Grant lavishly, and noticeably, on Fisk's yacht, thereby encouraging the perception that Grant's administration would support the pair's financial maneuvers.

By purchasing gold aggressively, Fisk and Gould were able to make the price of gold skyrocket over a period of four days—and send the nation into a financial crisis. When the President realized the intentions of the speculators, he ordered the Treasury Department to sell off $4 million in federal gold reserves. That step brought the price of gold down quickly, but it also brought ruin to many businesses and investors.

On Friday, September 24, 1869, as a result of the Fisk/Gould scheme and Grant's reaction to it, the nation underwent a severe economic shock comparable to the Wall Street stock market crash it would encounter 60 years later. Grant's judgment in associating so closely with Fisk and Gould was questioned, and his brother-in-law's influence within the White House was a matter of heated discussion.

The Credit Mobilier Affair

The second major scandal of the Grant Administration came to light during the President's 1872 reelection campaign, but did not prevent Grant's victory against newspaper publisher Horace Greeley.

Officials of the Credit Mobilier holding company had embezzled massive amounts of money during the construction of the Union Pacific Railroad, which had been subsidized by the federal government. In order to avoid being discovered, they tried to bribe members of Congress by selling them stock in the company at substantial discounts. High officials in the Republican party coordinated, and benefited from, the bribery campaign.

Abuse of delinquent tax collection authority

John D. Sanborn, a tax collector appointed by Grant's Treasury Department, worked under a corrupt fee structure that allowed him to keep one-half of the delinquent taxes he collected. An 1874 investigation by the House of Representatives demonstrated that Sanborn had collected more than $400,000 in back taxes, and had retained more than $200,000 as his compensation.

The Whiskey Ring

Grant's own treasury secretary, Benjamin H. Bristow, discovered massive levels of fraud and abuse among liquor distillers and the federal officials whose job it was to collect taxes from them. Millions of dollars in tax revenue due to the government were being diverted directly to the conspirators' own use. Upon being informed of the situation, Grant called for swift action against anyone found to be guilty, but when the President's trusted personal secretary, Orville Babcock, was suspected of having played a role in the tax diversions, the investigation ground to a halt. Nevertheless, 110 of the conspirators were found guilty.

The Belknap Bribery

In 1876, Secretary of War W.W. Belknap was shown to have been taking bribes from corrupt white traders at Indian posts. The payments had initially been channeled through Belknap's wife, but had, after her death, been paid directly to the secretary. The scandal was a deflating event for the Grant administration, which had made much of its earlier attempts to institute a fair and nonabusive set of policies toward the Indian tribes. Facing certain impeachment in the Senate, Belknap resigned his post.

Following, you will find the same text you just read, with one possible highlighting effort underlined. *The text you are about to read represents the result of a "skim-first-then-read-for-detail" approach.* Although you should not expect to have highlighted exactly the same entries that are marked in the following text, your study efforts will be most effective if you are in general agreement about what is—and is not—a key point.

The troubled Grant Administration: five scandals

Five major scandals tainted the administration of President Ulysses S. Grant. Although the hero of Vicksburg was the first chief executive to encounter serious, credible charges of substantial wrongdoing within his presidency, he himself was never convincingly associated with any direct involvement in criminal acts. The first of the five unsavory incidents came in 1869, the first year of the Civil War hero's presidency, and was known as Black Friday.

Black Friday

Speculators James Fisk and Jay Gould aimed to corner the gold market. They enlisted the assistance of the President's brother-in-law in an attempt to gain influence within the White House as it established the nation's financial policies, and hoped to prevent the government from "dumping" its gold onto the market, a step that would make their scheme impossible to carry out.

The two also entertained Grant lavishly, and noticeably, on Fisk's yacht, thereby encouraging the perception that Grant's administration would support the pair's financial maneuvers.

By purchasing gold aggressively, Fisk and Gould were able to make the price of gold skyrocket over a period of four days—and send the nation into a financial crisis. When the President realized the intentions of the speculators, he ordered the Treasury Department to sell off $4 million in federal gold reserves. That step brought the price of gold down quickly, but it also brought ruin to many businesses and investors.

On Friday, September 24, 1869, as a result of the Fisk/Gould scheme and Grant's reaction to it, the nation underwent a severe economic shock comparable to the Wall Street stock market crash it would encounter 60 years later. Grant's judgment in associating so closely with Fisk and Gould was questioned, and his brother-in-law's influence within the White House was a matter of heated discussion.

The Credit Mobilier Affair

The second major scandal of the Grant Administration came to light during the President's 1872 reelection campaign, but did not prevent Grant's victory against newspaper publisher Horace Greeley. Officials of the Credit Mobilier holding company had embezzled massive amounts of money during the construction of the Union Pacific Railroad, which had been subsidized by the federal government. In order to avoid being discovered, they tried to bribe members of Congress by selling them stock in the company at substantial discounts. High officials in the Republican party coordinated, and benefited from, the bribery campaign.

Abuse of delinquent tax collection authority

John D. Sanborn, a tax collector appointed by Grant's Treasury Department, worked under a corrupt fee structure that allowed him to keep one-half of the delinquent taxes he collected. An 1874 investigation by the

House of Representatives demonstrated that Sanborn had collected more than $400,000 in back taxes, and had retained more than $200,000 as his compensation.

The Whiskey Ring

Grant's own treasury secretary, Benjamin H. Bristow, discovered massive levels of fraud and abuse among liquor distillers and the federal officials whose job it was to collect taxes from them. Millions of dollars in tax revenue due to the government were being diverted directly to the conspirators' own use. Upon being informed of the situation, Grant called for swift action against anyone found to be guilty—but when the President's trusted personal secretary, Orville Babcock, was suspected of having played a role in the tax diversions, the investigation ground to a halt. Nevertheless, 110 of the conspirators were found guilty.

The Belknap Bribery

In 1876, Secretary of War W.W. Belknap was shown to have been taking bribes from corrupt white traders at Indian posts. The payments had initially been channeled through Belknap's wife, but had, after her death, been paid directly to the secretary. The scandal was a deflating event for the Grant administration, which had made much of its earlier attempts to institute a fair and nonabusive set of policies toward the Indian tribes. Facing certain impeachment in the Senate, Belknap resigned his post.

How do you know when you're ready to move on to the next portion of the material you're studying? If you've written or highlighted definitions of key terms, developed questions and accompanying answers that make the topic clearer for you and developed questions for which you don't have the answer to bear in mind as you continue your study time, it's a good bet you're ready to move on.

Commit your highlighting efforts to new, "compressed" written notes. Whether you are reading a textbook or highlighting your own notes from class, you should develop an outline of important points, based on your reading, reviewing for detail and highlighting work.

Here's what the Ulysses S. Grant material you just read would look like when committed to a new, abbreviated written outline. (Note the heavy use of appropriate abbreviations, most of which are achieved by simply omitting needless vowels. These are techniques you should incorporate into your classroom note-taking work as well.)

Grant: 5 scandals

G not drctly tied to any crms

1. *Black Friday*
   a. Fisk, Gould, specultrs: aimed t crnr gold mkt. Hoped t prvnt govt fm "dmpng" gold onto mkt
   b. Encrgd prcption G admin spprted maneuvers
   c. G finally figured out what was up; ordered Treasry to sll $4m in gold
   d. 9/24/1869 (Blk Frdy), svre economic shck rslts

2. *Credit Mobilier Affair*
   a Hppnd drg 1872 reelec camp.; didn't prvnt G victory against Horace Greeley.
   b. C.M. Hldng co. embezzled big $ during cnstrctn UP RR, tried to use stock to bribe mems of Cong. to keep fm being xposd

3. *Delinquent tax collection abuse*
   a. John D. Sanborn, tx cllctr w/G's Treasury Dept, kept ½ all $—200 grand on 400 grand cllctd!
   b. 1874 Cong. investigation discovered.

4. *Whiskey Ring*
   a. G's Treasury Sec., Benjamin H. Bristow, found mjr fraud, abuse among liquor distillers and feds cllctg txes. G vows action.
   b. G's own prsnl sect'y, Orville Babcock, implctd; invstg'tn then stymied.
   c. 110 convictns.

5. *Belknap Bribery*
   a. 1876, Sec'y War W.W. Belknap found taking bribes fm corrupt wht trdrs @ Indian posts.
   b. When impchmnt in Senate a lock, Belknap rsgnd.

Review, review, review. You've still got some days on the calendar to work with, so use that to your advantage. Schedule in times for periodic review of your study material. Repetition now can mean good grades on the test, as can *reciting important materials out loud.*

Develop a Power List

One to two days before the test, prepare—and reinforce—an appropriate Power List covering the key points of the material. What's a Power List? It's the natural culmination of the acronym, replacement/exaggeration and numeric sounds techniques you learned in the previous chapter. It can be expanded or contracted as you see fit, and can accommodate whatever materials you feel are important to review. Developing a Power List is not a substitute for studying your material, but a convenient way to memorize key points that you can later reconstruct—on paper, if that's an option—during the test.

If you have the three strategies from the previous chapter down, and if you've effectively highlighted your written text and taken good notes, you're ready to supercharge your study and memorization efforts. Here's how:

Step 1

Develop an *acronym* appropriate to the material you've been studying. In the case of the misdeeds that occurred within the Grant administration, you'd probably want one that reminds you of Grant himself *and* of each of the five main scandals:

1. Black Friday
2. Credit Mobilier Affair
3. Delinquent tax collection abuse
4. Whiskey Ring
5. Belknap Bribery

President Grant smoked a lot of cigars; he died of throat cancer as a result of the habit. Let's use the CIGAR to represent Grant and his administration.

Take a look at this acronym:

*C*alendar
*I*nvestments
*G*ratuity
*A*lcohol
*R*edskins (football team)

Developing an acronym along these lines is the first step in building your Power List. (Please note, however, that the acronym itself is a powerful memory tool, and you should certainly feel free to use something along the lines of the one we've just constructed if you feel uncomfortable working with the Power List techniques you're about to learn.)

Now, you'll have to take my word for the fact that I chose the word "cigar" for two reasons: because it reminded me of President Grant, and because it has five letters, corresponding *in number* to the five main points in the material we just reviewed. As far as content goes, the following connections to the five main points of the passage were the result of a little inspired manipulation with words. Similarly on-target associations could have been developed from just about *any* word that met the initial criteria.

The acronym you develop *is not supposed to do the entire job*. It is simply to remind you of the key points in your condensed notes.

Calendar, representing the "C" in "cigar," serves as a springboard to remind me of the only one of Grant's scandals that is related to a particular day—Black Friday. But the word "calendar" doesn't offer me any of the particulars about Black Friday. It's not supposed to.

Investments, representing the "I" in "cigar," reminds me that stocks were used as a means to attempt to bribe federal officials in the Credit Mobilier affair. But the single word "investments" certainly doesn't make the cumbersome phrase "Credit Mobilier" any easier to remember or point me toward the specifics of that scandal.

The word *gratuity,* meaning gift or extra payment, certainly applies to the healthy commissions to which tax collector John Sanborn helped himself in the third scandal. But it doesn't tell me how much, or in what capacity he took his gratuities.

Alcohol, which corresponds to the "A" in "cigar," serves as a reminder that the fourth scandal involved distillers, but it doesn't tell me much more than that.

And *Redskins*, while it refers initially to the Washington, D.C., sports franchise, alerts me to the fact that the fifth and final scandal I need to remember about the Grant Administration had to do with corruption at Indian trading posts. Beyond that, it conveys no meaningful information.

These initial connections will serve as the foundation for separate memory chains that will provide all the detail about the particular topics they describe. The Power List acronym's only job is to remind you of the main subject headings from your notes.

Step 2

Form a memory chain from each word in your acronym.

Let's look at those condensed notes once again, with the initial ideas of our acronym inserted appropriately:

Grant: 5 scandals [CIGAR]

G not drctly tied to any crms

1. *Black Friday [CALENDAR]*
   a. Fisk, Gould, specultrs: aimed t crnr gold mkt. Hoped t prvnt govt fm "dmpng" gold onto mkt
   b. Encrgd prception G admin spprted maneuvers
   c. G finally figured out what was up; ordered Treasry to sll $4m in gold
   d. 9/24/1869 (Blk Frdy), svre economic shck rslts
2. *Credit Mobilier Affair [INVESTMENTS]*
   a. Hppnd drg 1872 reelec camp.; didn't prvnt G victory against Horace Greeley.
   b. C.M. Hldng co. embezzled big $ during cnstrctn U.P. RR, tried to use stock to bribe mems of Cong. to keep fm being xposd
3. *Delinquent Tax Collection Abuse [GRATUITY]*
   a. John D. Sanborn, tx cllctr w/G's Treasury Dept, kept ½ all $—200 grand on 400 grand cllctd!
   b. 1874 Cong. investigation discovered.
4. *Whiskey Ring [ALCOHOL]*
   a. G's Treasury Sec., Benjamin H. Bristow, found mjr fraud, abuse among liquor distillers and feds cllctg txes. G vows action.
   b. G's own prsnl sect'y, Orville Babcock, implctd; invstg'tn then stymied.
   c. 110 convictns.

5. *Belknap Bribery [REDSKINS]*
   a. 1876, Sec'y War W.W. Belknap found taking bribes fm corrupt wht trdrs @ Indian posts.
   b. When impchmnt in Senate a lock, Belknap rsgnd.

Please remember that the very act of committing images to the ideas in your notes, as we're about to do, will help your "natural" retention. Even if the images I suggest (which are no replacements for the ones you develop on your own) seem elaborate to you at first, they will nevertheless help you remember and reinforce the basic concepts you highlighted in your study material.

The initial image—Grant's *cigar*—will, of course, be our entry to this Power List. When it comes time to think of the scandals of the Grant administration, we'll picture one of Grant's vices, something that turned out to be dangerous to him—his cigar-smoking habit—and that image will serve as a reminder of the other vices we've been studying that relate to Grant, namely the unmistakable whiff of corruption around his presidency.

So much for the initial connection. What about the rest of the facts within the condensed notes? Well, the first to deal with is one of the most essential points in the material we read: The fact that Grant himself was never convincingly connected in a direct way to any of the crimes associated with his term in office. We're going to connect this *introductory point* not to any element of the Power List acronym, but to the *image with which that acronym presents us.* This way, if we remember nothing else, we'll remember something vital from the initial part of our scan-and-review process: Although there were serious scandals within the Grant administration, the President himself was never directly implicated in any of them.

In your Power List, connect one or more critical introductory ideas to the image of your acronym itself. (You see now, I'm sure, the benefit of selecting an acronym with a powerful, picture-oriented word or phrase as its main thrust!)

Here's one way we might connect the introductory idea to the acronym:

> *President Grant is smoking a massive cigar—easily five feet long—in front of the White House. He drops the unwieldy cigar, and a huge fire sets in, from the lawn where he smoked, and upward toward the Executive Mansion itself. Flames consume the entire building and all the grounds, right up to the place where Grant was standing, but the general is untouched by the blackened ruins that now surround him.*

Untouched by flame and destruction—untouched by scandal. The connection is strong enough to work for *me;* if there's a better one that will do the job for *you,* you should certainly feel free to make it.

If you had three or four introductory ideas to incorporate at the beginning of your Power List, you would simply connect "fire" to the next idea on the list to develop a brand new image, in accordance with the ideas set forth in the previous chapter. Remember the layout of a memory chain?

(By the way, if you have more than three big introductory ideas to memorize in this way, there's a good chance your organization of the study facts you're working with could be more streamlined.)

From this point, developing the Power List is simply a matter of developing (in this case) five "free-standing" memory chains, each of which uses as its initial image one of the words from the CIGAR acronym. Here's my go at the material, but bear in mind that the connections that work for me may not be the same as the ones that work for you. What follows is, however, in keeping with the ideas of replacement and exaggeration we discussed in the previous chapter and should serve as a good model for your own development of Power Lists.

Grant: 5 scandals [CIGAR]

G not drctly tied to any crms

1. *Black Friday [CALENDAR]*

[*CALENDAR* to *BLACK FRIDAY*: You're *frying* a *calendar* on the stove until it turns smoky and *black*. Smell the smoke!]

a. Fisk, Gould, specultrs: aimed t crnr gold mkt. Hoped t prvnt govt fm "dmpng" gold onto mkt

[*BLACK FRIDAY* to *GOULD, FISK CORNERING* GOLD MARKET:

[You're *frying* a mass of *black* foul-smelling *goo*; the more you heat it, the worse it smells. (Imagine the smell of burning rubber.) You try to put the stench out by plunging your *fist* into the *corner* of the hot pan—it burns!]*

(My approach here is to avoid altogether the temptation to memorize the word "gold"—it's too similar to "Gould," which I've rendered here as goo, a word not likely to be mistaken for "gold." The image of the corner of the pan will remind us that Fisk and Gould were out to corner the market—as will, of course, our earlier review of the material!)

[GOULD, FISK CORNERING GOLD MARKET to HOPED TO KEEP GOVERNMENT FROM DUMPING:]

Note: There's no need to use *every* aspect of the previous image in continuing your chain; I find that something like the following works quite well.

[You are pelting handfuls of foul-smelling *goo* at the president of the United States! Why? He's getting ready to *dump* garbage in your living room—in fact, he's driven a garbage truck through the wall, and is preparing to eject its contents right in front of you—and you want to *keep* him from doing this! (You're better off imagining the current occupant of the White House, or whatever personal embodiment of the government carries the strongest associations for you, rather than President Grant.)]

b. Encrgd prcption G admin spprted maneuvers [HOPED TO KEEP GOVERNMENT FROM DUMPING to HOPED TO CONVINCE OTHERS GOVERNMENT SUPPORTED MANEUVERS:]

It may not seem that a single striking word or image can do the trick when it comes to encompassing an idea like this one—but if the image you select is one that works for *you*, you'll be surprised at how much information the image can convey. Your aim is not to reproduce your study material verbatim, but to develop mental "triggers" that will point you toward your "natural" memory of that material.

[The President (government) has backed a garbage truck into your living room (dump)—and suddenly camera crews are everywhere! You demand that the President support you financially for the rest of your life, and he refuses. In order to convince the reporters of your need, you start eating all the garbage from the truck. Picture each item as you eat it!]

c. G finally figured out what was up; ordered Treasry to sll $4m in gold

[HOPED TO *CONVINCE* OTHERS GOVERNMENT *SUPPORTED* MANEUVERS to *TREASURY* SELLS *$4M* IN *GOLD*:]

[You're eating garbage in front of reporters and camera crews in order to convince them of your need for financial support. One of the newspeople (make it your own favorite news anchor) decides that enough is enough, and produces a treasure chest the size of a house (Treasury Department), opens it up, and starts shoving a huge solid-gold ear down your throat. (The big gold "ear," of course, translates to $4 million in gold. See the picture. Feel the metal in your throat. Maybe it makes you choke a little bit!)]

d. 9/24/1869 (Blk Frdy), svre economic shck rslts
[*TREASURY* SELLS *$4M* IN *GOLD* to *ECONOMIC SHOCK* ON *9/24/69* (BLACK FRIDAY):]

[Someone has shoved a gold ear down your throat—it's half in and half out. To dislodge it, you head over to an electric socket and stick the ear into it. You get a shock, of course, a very severe one, but you spit the gold statue into an open warship (9/24/69)—a battleship with the top sawed right off—that is sailing past you in midair. Hear the clink of metal against metal as you finally dislodge the statue from your throat.]

2. *Credit Mobilier Affair [INVESTMENTS]*
[*INVESTMENTS* to *CREDIT MOBILIER*:]
This is a particularly important link in the chain—it must effectively remind you of that strange name!

[You're at a dinner party. You are wearing a gigantic vest (investments) that is made entirely of credit cards—feel the edges cut sharply into your sides. It's very uncomfortable, so you take it off and hang it from the ceiling, where it revolves slowly. It's such a beautiful mobile that, fortunately for you, no one at the party notices that you're now stark naked!]

I would avoid the temptation to make the credit cards "Mobil" gasoline cards. There's no particular exaggeration to this image—it's entirely too logical. From this point onward, the credit card can serve as your mental shorthand for "Credit Mobilier."

a. Hppnd drg 1872 reelec camp.; didn't prvnt G victory against Horace Greeley.

[*CREDIT* MOBILIER to *1872*/STILL *BEAT GREELEY*:]

[You're trying to use a billboard-sized credit card to pay for a TV canoe (1872)—see it there on the sales counter, a full-sized canoe with a big color television built right into the front. But the saleslady won't sell the canoe to you...so you pick up the canoe and beat her with it. That doesn't do the trick, so you pour hot grease (Greeley) on her hand...and she finally accepts payment.]

b. C.M. Hldng co. embezzled big $ during cnstrctn U.P. RR, tried to use stock to bribe mems of Cong. to keep fm being xposd

[*1872*/STILL *BEAT GREELEY* to *RAILROAD EMBEZZLEMENT*, THEN *STOCK BRIBES* TO TRY TO *KEEP CONGRESSMEN QUIET*:]

[You're paddling along a river, watching TV in your special canoe, when a huge locomotive speeds through, cutting the canoe in half! An incredibly long arm extends from the train and picks your pocket (embezzlement) as the train whizzes through the water, then disappears. You try to grasp a flower stalk (stock bribes) to keep from drowning, but Newt

Gingrich (or whoever helps you remember Congress) plucks it first and tries to tape it over his own mouth, without much success (quiet).]

3. *Delinquent tax collection abuse [GRATUITY]*
   [*GRATUITY* to *LATE TAX* COLLECTION:]

[At a restaurant, you pay for your check in cash, but leave your tip (gratuity) by using thumbtacks (tax) to attach a ringing alarm clock (lateness) to your waiter. He doesn't appreciate it much!]

   a. John D. Sanborn, tx cllctr w/G's Treasury Dept, kept ½ all $—200 grand on 400 grand cllctd!
   [*LATE TAX* COLLECTION to *SANBORN* GETS *HALF*:]

[Picture yourself trying to tack that ringing alarm clock (late taxes) into the sand (Sanborn) at the beach. As you do so, the noisy clock splits neatly in half (50 percent commission), right down the middle!]

   b. 1874 Cong. investigation discovered.
   [*SANBORN* GETS *HALF* to *1874 CONGRESSIONAL INVESTIGATION* DISCOVERS THE ABUSES:]

[While digging around in the beach sand (Sanborn) with a tough crow (1874—picture this strange beach toy as a dead bird!), you expose the Capitol Building itself (congressional investigation), which is beneath the beach for some reason!)]

4. *Whiskey Ring [ALCOHOL]*
   [*ALCOHOL* to WHISKEY *RING:]*

[You're in your own bathroom drinking a container of rubbing alcohol straight from the bottle—it's so disgusting that you decide, instead of swallowing it, to spit it out into your bathtub, and use the alcohol to scrub away the ring you see there.]

a. G's Treasury Sec., Benjamin H. Bristow, found mjr fraud, abuse among liquor distillers and feds cllctg txes. G vows action.

[WHISKEY *RING* to *BRISTOW FINDS ABUSE*:]

[You're scrubbing away at your bathtub ring with a brisket of beef—which starts talking back to you about dirt that it's found (finds abuse), dirt that you haven't scrubbed out yet!]

b. G's own prsnl sect'y, Orville Babcock, implctd; invstg'tn then stymied.

[*BRISTOW FINDS ABUSE* to *BABCOCK* INVOLVED, *INVESTIGATION STOPS*:]

[You use your brisket of beef to try to shut up someone who's babbling (Babcock)—picture yourself whacking the most talkative person you know right in the kisser with the brisket as he or she speaks! The person keeps talking, though, and starts screaming about starting an investigation into the incident. See yourself extending a hand right onto the person's mouth and holding the lips closed with your fingers—the talk of an investigation stops.]

c. 110 convictns.

[*BABCOCK* INVOLVED, *INVESTIGATION STOPS* to *110 CONVICTIONS*:]

[Picture the babbling person in tights (110)—and nothing else! The sight is so absurd that you have no recourse but to summon a policeman, who throws this person in jail (convictions).]

5. *Belknap bribery [REDSKINS]*
   [*REDSKINS* to *BELKNAP* BRIBERY]

[Picture yourself playing football (Redskins) with a huge school *bell* (Belknap), the kind the principal might ring when recess comes to an end. You're dragging the bell across your face, using it to smear eyeblack every which way. Your face is, not surprisingly, a mess—you can tell as you look in the mirror that yours is not the neatest makeup job in the world!]

a. 1876, Sec'y War W.W. Belknap found taking bribes fm corrupt wht trdrs @ Indian posts.
   [*BELKNAP* to *BRIBES FROM* CORRUPT *TRADERS*:]

[You're ringing your bell right in the ear of Daniel Boone [trader], and it's so loud that he starts weeping right in front of you. Finally, he gives you a 100-dollar bill [bribes] to stop.]

b. When impchmnt in Senate a lock, Belknap rsgnd.
   [*BRIBES FROM* CORRUPT *TRADERS* to *FACING IMPEACHMENT*, RESIGNS.]

[See yourself holding a huge peach, one roughly the size of a watermelon, and grinding it slowly into Daniel Boone's [trader's] face.]

If you take the time to develop and, just as important, *repeat and reinforce* each of the images in your Power List, you will soon be able to reconstitute highlights from your condensed notes on paper, from memory and in the proper sequence, at any time you wish. Simply begin with the first picture you linked to Grant's CIGAR—the flames around the White House that left him untouched.

Grant: 5 scandals

PRESIDENT HIMSELF NEVER DIRECTLY LINKED TO CRIMINAL ACTS

BLACK FRIDAY

- GOULD, FISK CORNERING GOLD MARKET
- HOPED TO KEEP GOVERNMENT FROM DUMPING
- HOPED TO CONVINCE OTHERS GOVERNMENT SUPPORTED MANEUVERS
- TREASURY SELLS $4M IN GOLD
- ECONOMIC SHOCK ON 9/24/69 (BLACK FRIDAY)

CREDIT MOBILIER

- 1872/STILL BEAT GREELEY
- RAILROAD EMBEZZLEMENT, THEN STOCK BRIBES TO TRY TO KEEP CONGRESSMEN QUIET

LATE TAX COLLECTION

- SANBORN GETS HALF
- 1874 CONGRESSIONAL INVESTIGATION DISCOVERS THE ABUSES

WHISKEY RING

- BRISTOW FINDS ABUSE
- BABCOCK INVOLVED, INVESTIGATION STOPS
- 110 CONVICTIONS

BELKNAP BRIBERY

- BRIBES FROM CORRUPT TRADERS
- FACING IMPEACHMENT, RESIGNS

A few important notes on the Power List technique are in order before we move on:

- **A Power List is no substitute for reading and reviewing the study material.** It will remind you of points you have studied, but it will not make you the master of material you have *not* studied. If you try to develop pictures and mnemonic material for material you have not taken the time to familiarize yourself with, you will not do well on the test! Read first; memorize afterwards.
- **Remember to review your Power List images several times before you attempt to use the list in a test.** Don't get discouraged if you miss a few the first time around. Go back and strengthen whichever associations got past you the first time.
- **Be creative: Adapt the system to your own needs and abilities.** Nothing is written in stone here! The Power List relating to the scandals of the Grant administration that I just laid out goes into detail, primarily because I want you to be able to use this powerful memory tool for as many situations as possible, and because a detailed Power List is the one for which people often need the most guidance. You may decide to scale back the level of detail for your own needs. Remember, the memory system that works for *you* is the one that's "correct."
- **Some people don't like working with Power Lists.** That's okay. They *can* be a little intimidating at first. Remember that the goal is simply to allow you to reproduce your condensed notes, on paper

and from memory, before starting in on the test. Give the method a fair shake, but if it doesn't seem to be your cup of tea, stick with the three basic memory techniques outlined in Chapters 3 and 4. (For another, considerably simpler, memorization technique that will allow you to reproduce key notes before or during a test, see Chapter 7.)

Budget your time during the test!

If questions or sections are weighted, be sure that you leave yourself plenty of time for the parts of the test that count the most. It's best to leave nothing blank, of course, but if you have to abandon some part of the exam, it's better to do a superb job on three sections that count for 90 percent of your grade than on two that count for 10 percent of your grade.

Chapter 6

If you have a test in 6 to 9 days

You say you've got a week or so in which to prepare for a forthcoming exam? Your first step should be to follow the advice in Chapter 2 and develop a written plan for attacking the various aspects of the work you will face in the coming days.

Prioritize!

You should use your Planning Calendar, your weekly Priority Task Sheet and your Daily Schedule to help you establish key goals and make the most intelligent use possible of the time available before the test. Identify those portions of the exam that are the most important to prepare for and grant them highest priority.

Do your level best to schedule your test preparation activities during your own personal "prime time." Store all your planning materials in your Study Plan Central book. Take time out each day to chart your progress toward the most important goals you've identified for yourself.

"What do I do when?"

Take a look at the following suggested outline of the major study issues you could choose to focus on in the time available to you. This outline assumes that you have eight days to work with. Understand that this breakdown is only a rough guide, one that you should not attempt to follow exactly. Your situation is unique; your own "prime time," class commitments, scheduling issues and work responsibilities will dictate that you customize this basic schedule to your own requirements. You should, however, make an effort to hit all of the basic research and preparation steps outlined here.

- **Days 8 to 7:** Pull out all the written materials appropriate to the test. Tackle the most important ones first, and review them for key points. (If you are tempted to read all of the materials word-for-word, see the advice on skimming and reading for detail that appears in Chapter 5.)
- **Days 6 to 5:** Review your class notes. Develop a set of condensed notes. (See Chapter 5.)
- **Days 5 to 3:** Organize a study group. Develop strategies for likely exam questions. Try to obtain previous exams from your instructor.
- **Part of Day 2:** Consult the test-taking strategies that appear in Chapter 13.
- **Remainder of Day 2, and all of Day 1:** Construct a Power List that covers all the key points you've been studying over the past few days. Instructions on developing a Power List appear in Chapter 5, but if you decide that this memorization technique is not for you, take a look at the simplified memorization system outlined in Chapter 8. This may be better suited to your needs.
- **The morning of the test:** Practice transferring your memorized notes to paper without benefit of any study materials. This "reinforcement" stage

(which you should practice earlier in the process, as well) will help you reconstruct the material you need when test time rolls around. If you find you can reconstruct the most recent draft of your notes without too much trouble, you may decide that it makes sense to transfer them all to paper—quickly and accurately, of course—during the exam. This will afford easy reference to the main materials and concepts you've studied.

Plan your work, work your plan

It's worth repeating: Making the most of your personal "prime time" is an important part of winning the best possible grade on your exam. If you can't make your scheduled study time correspond precisely to a time when you're most likely to be "on," you must still study, of course—but you should avoid at all costs spending most of your time studying when you know you're exhausted, ineffective or both.

Making the most effective use of your available time also means briefly reviewing the various tasks on your priority list, then going back for more detail later. You will almost certainly be wasting your precious time if you attempt to march syllable-by-syllable through each and every line of all your study materials. If you get a good sense of the material before you proceed to your detailed study work, you'll reduce the likelihood of coming across something that's completely unfamiliar to you when making your way through the actual exam.

As the days pass and the test approaches, don't exhaust yourself in a vain attempt to master every possible topic that may appear on the exam. It's more important to show up coherent, well-nourished and well-rested than it is to attempt to develop a top-to-bottom "knowledge" of the subject that you will not be able to reproduce at exam time.

Remember: The shorter the time frame you're working with, the more important it is that you take good care of yourself. Don't forget to eat. Don't forget to sleep. Don't get distracted by social events. Stay away from drugs. Stay away from alcohol.

And during the test itself...

Budget your available time sensibly. Determine which parts of the exam, if any, are weighted more heavily than other parts; allot more of your time and attention to those sections than to less critical parts of the test.

Chapter 7

If you have a test in 2 to 5 days

Cutting it close, eh? Well, before you do anything, remember that people who are frightened don't study very well. So Step One is: Don't panic! Once you've fully committed yourself to this sound goal, you should proceed to Step Two, which is as follows:

Set up your battle plan

What you need is a detailed plan that would make General Patton proud. Use your Planning Calendar, your weekly Priority Task Sheet and your Daily Schedule to set up a plan that will ensure that you cover all the essential points...and still have a few brain cells left when test time arrives. Store all the appropriate record-keeping materials in your Study Plan Central book.

If at all possible, you should find a way to use most, if not all, of your own personal "prime time"—the time when you get your best work done—preparing for the test. Work hard, but take brief breaks at the end of each day to monitor your progress toward key goals. Such "how'm I doing?" breaks will help you spot any important study areas you may have overlooked. You can also use these "update" periods to identify all the parts of your study plan that are working, which is certainly a nice boost during crunch time.

One way to plan your time

Here's a suggested breakdown of the way you could decide to schedule the time available to you. It assumes that you have five days to prepare for the exam. This is not the only way to go, of course. The plan you develop will have to incorporate circumstances such as work schedules, class time and the like. But this plan should serve as a good model for a first draft of a customized plan that will work for you.

- **Day 5:** Review all written materials!. Don't try to read every line of every textbook; do skim and review as outlined in Chapter 5.
- **Day 4 and part of Day 3:** Go over your own written notes from the class; develop a set of condensed notes. See Chapter 5 for advice on setting up these notes.
- **Remainder of Day 3:** Spend some time in a study group. Keep the focus on strategies for dealing with the most likely exam questions. If you can, track down a copy of an old exam from the instructor; use it as the basis of a group discussion.
- **Part of Day 2:** Read or reread Chapter 13. It features some important advice on exam strategy.
- **Remainder of Day 2 and all of Day 1:** Memorize the key concepts and study points you've identified over the past few days. You can either use the comprehensive Power List approach that is discussed in Chapter 5, or the easier-to-master system discussed in Chapter 8. Whichever technique of memorization you decide to use, remember that reinforcement after you've made your initial associations and images is a critical part of any memorizing job.

- **The morning of the test:** Review your written notes one last time. Test your memorized materials: Can you reproduce them accurately without appealing to any of your study materials? If you can, you may want to consider reproducing them quickly and accurately during the test for reference.

Stuff to remember as you get ready for the exam

Use your personal "prime time" wisely! If you really want to get the best possible grade on the test, it's imperative that you do as much study work as possible during that part of the day when you know you do the best work. Granted, you may not be able to make your scheduled study time correspond exactly to the slot when you're likely to do your best work, and you must still find some time to study if that time is unavailable for some reason. But you should make heroic efforts to free up even modest chunks of your schedule over the next few days if doing so will yield more productive "on" time for your test preparation campaign.

Remember that the objective, at least at first, is to briefly review the various items on your priority list. You can go back for more detail later on the most important items. Don't start on the first page of your textbook and spend hours analyzing the introduction for every scrap of meaning it may possess. The idea is to get a sense of the broad outlines of the material before you, then deepen your understanding. If you do this, you'll find you've reduced the number of topics that will throw you for a complete loop during the exam.

Don't kill yourself getting ready for the test. You probably can't master every possible aspect of the topic before you. Make a point of arriving at the test site rested, nourished and relatively coherent. The less time you have to prepare for your test, the more important it is to treat yourself well and avoid energy-consuming (and time-consuming!) distractions. Keep your social engagements brief during this period, and don't get sidetracked by them. Avoid drinking alcohol. Don't do any drugs.

During the exam...

Use your time intelligently. Take a few moments at the beginning of the test to make some rough guesses about how much time you should allocate to each component. Are there any parts of the exam that are weighted more heavily than the rest? If so, you should allot more of your time and attention to those parts than you do to less critical elements. In a perfect world, of course, you wouldn't leave *anything* blank, but if you have to skip something, wouldn't you prefer it to be a portion of the test that represents 20 percent, rather than 80 percent, of your final grade?

Chapter 8

If you have to take the test *tomorrow*

So you're really under the gun. Not to worry.

Worry is only going to cost you mental energy, so skip it. You're going to do the best job you possibly can, within the time constraints you face. That job *starts* with planning your time before you start studying.

"But there's only one day! Shouldn't I get right to work, instead of wasting time setting up a plan?" The *less* time you have, the *more* important it is to use that time sensibly.

Follow the advice in Chapter 2. Develop a written battle plan, *even if the test is tomorrow!* You have a lot to get done in a very short period of time, so you must schedule your test preparation activities carefully. Isolate the most important elements of the exam you must prepare for, and give them the highest priority. Schedule the most important work for your own personal "prime time." Keep all appropriate notes in your Study Plan Central book.

Needless to say, time is at a premium now; don't try to work line-by-line through your study materials. Take a few moments now to review or reacquaint yourself with the ideas in Chapter 5 on skimming and highlighting.

Relax. Your worst potential enemy now is not the study material, but your own mental attitude toward it. Keep your mind free and open, and if you feel yourself panicking or tightening up, *stop what you're doing immediately* and find some way to blow off a little steam. You will be using your mind a lot over the next few hours. Treat it nicely. Feed it. Give it occasional breaks. When it's done all it can do, *let it sleep* before you expect it to make sense of an exam.

If "cramming" means staying up all night to review material you're too tired to absorb, *don't cram!* Your main objective now is to review your text and/or notes for important points, acquaint yourself with as much of this material as you can, and *leave yourself some brain cells for the test tomorrow!*

Prepare a Power List covering the key points of the material. See the advice on highlighting and memorization that appears in Chapter 5. Obviously, you won't be able to cover things in *quite* the detail you would if you had a little more time at your disposal, but you *should* be able to develop images that will help you recall:

- Headings and topic sentences from your textbook.
- Important names and dates.
- Formulas and ratios.

If you have to choose between having a *good* grasp of a *limited* amount of material, or a *weak* grasp of a *lot* of material, opt for the first, and build from there!

Whatever you do, get a good night's sleep before the test. Eat sensibly. Stay away from drugs, alcohol and other distractions.

You don't have time to master the intricacies of the Power List?

Here's a quick and dirty alternative that will help you memorize lots of key points in a hurry. It's called *the alphabet.* The beauty of this bare-bones memory system is that you already know it. Here's a list of words, each of which sounds like the letter of the alphabet it represents. Take a look.

A: Ace Ventura	J: Jail	S: Essay
B: Beer	K: Cake	T: Tea
C: Sea	L: Hell	U: Ewe
D: Dean	M: Emerald	V: Veal
E: Eel	N: Enemy	W: Double chin
F: F. Lee Bailey	O: Oar	X: X-Ray
G: Jeans	P: Peel	Y: Wine
H: Agent	Q: Cueball	Z: Zebra
I: Eye	R: Army	

Talk about a list that practically memorizes itself! Read the alphabet list over once or twice silently; then read it *out loud* twice; then try to commit it to paper without looking at the book.

You now have 26 images you can use to memorize the 26 most important facts and principles from your notes and/or textbook review session. (Take the time to put these in rough order of importance, on paper, before you try to memorize them.)

Now, let's say you had to memorize this material:

Two early scandals in the administration of Ulysses S. Grant were Black Friday and the Credit Mobilier affair.

Let's assume that you have an intuitive grasp of the most important events of these two scandals. With one day to go before the test, you might choose to start out by memorizing the names themselves, one per letter. The first two letters of the alphabet might look like this:

ACE VENTURA to BLACK FRIDAY: (Can you picture Jim Carrey, in all his pet-detective glory, painting your calendar black—by applying the paint with his tongue? Can you picture yourself frying your calendar in a pan to get the paint off?)

BEER to CREDIT MOBILIER: (Imagine a long, tall, glass of beer—with credit cards floating in the bottom! See yourself drinking it down, cards and all. How does your throat feel?)

By isolating the 26 most important pieces of information in your notes, textbooks and other study materials, reading them *out loud,* then associating each with the appropriate key word representing a letter of the alphabet, you'll be able to prepare for the questions you're most likely to encounter on the test.

And once you show up for the test...

Be sure to budget your time wisely. Take a moment or two at the beginning of the process to determine which parts of the exam (if any) are weighted more heavily than others. Your first choice, of course, will be to avoid leaving any part of the test blank, but if you have to skip something, you'll want it to be a part of the test that has less bearing on your final grade than something else.

Chapter 9

If your paper is due in 10 to 15 days

Set up a battle plan, using the ideas and forms laid out in Chapter 2, then follow the Ron Fry hit-all-the-marks, no-frills, write-a-great-paper-in-the-time-you've-got system. There are 13 (lucky) components to this system, which you should map out with appropriate reference to and entries on your Planning Calendar, your weekly Priority Task Sheet and your Daily Schedule. Use these tools to allocate the time available to prepare your paper.

The 13 steps of my paper-writing system are:

Step 1: Choose a great topic—preferably one that both you *and* your instructor think is a magnificent selection.

Step 2: Head to the library for your initial research. Look at the resources available to you and make some initial notes on topics and references. Develop a "temporary thesis"—a central argument you will attempt to prove (or disprove) in your paper.

Step 3: Based on your initial research, prepare a general (very broad, very brief) outline. I call this a "temporary" outline. Don't spend too much time on it.

Step 4: Do *detailed* library research.

a. Set up a 3 x 5 card collection citing every article, book or other source you may use or make reference to in your paper. Number all these cards 1-R (for Reference), 2-R, 3-R, etc.

b. Commit *each* idea in your one-page outline to *another* set of 3 x 5 cards. Number all these cards 1-O (for Outline), 2-O, 3-O, etc. Add more 3 x 5 cards as your research requires. *Make sure each card isolates only one idea, fact or quote per card.* Never carry a single idea over to a second card.

Step 5: Shuffle the outline cards around until they form a coherent, detailed outline. Then commit that outline to paper.

Step 6: Hit the typewriter, computer, word processor or notepad—whichever you work best on—and use your card-based outline to develop a first draft of your paper.

Step 7: Do more research if necessary. Most of us come across gaps or new questions in the process of writing a first draft. This is your opportunity to use your library research time to tie up any loose research ends.

Step 8: Develop a second draft of your paper. Use your note cards to develop your bibliography.

Step 9: Proofread meticulously. (If you're using a computer or word processor, use the spell-check application.)

Step 10: Get someone *else* to proofread your paper meticulously. *Don't skip this step!* Computer spell-checks don't catch everything, and you are too close to the material now to catch every spelling or grammar problem.

Step 11: Incorporate the changes from Steps 9 and 10 in a final draft. Make sure the final output is *clean, neat and in complete conformity with your teacher's specifications.* No matter what your instructor says, neatness really does count—sometimes for far more than it should!

Step 12: *Carefully* proofread your paper one final time. Do not leave smudges or stains. If the paper looks less than sharp, start all over again and set up another draft!

Step 13: Have you followed your teacher's instructions to the letter? Is the paper clean and attractive? Have you kept at least one copy of the paper for your own records?

Let's assume that you have 12 days at your disposal to work on your paper, not counting the day that the paper is actually due. Here's a *recommended* breakdown of how you can use the scheduling tools we discussed in Chapter 2 to allocate your time according to this 13-step plan.

Days 12 and 11: Determine the topic and "angle" of your paper. (Steps 1 through 3.)

Day 10: Develop a list of references. (Step 4.)

Days 9 to 6: Read your reference materials; take notes; compose your detailed outline; write your first draft. (Steps 5 and 6.)

Days 5 to 3: Do additional research if necessary; develop the second draft and edit the paper; prepare your bibliography/list of sources. (Steps 7 and 8.)

Days 2 to 1: Proofread the paper; print or type the final copy. (Steps 9 through 13.)

Before you try to start writing your first draft, review the note cards closely; think about the ways the various ideas might fit together in a paragraph. Rearrange the cards into the order that seems most appropriate for the paragraph in question; repeat the process for each batch of cards in your outline.

During your library research, check the *Reader's Guide to Periodical Literature* for appropriate article citations on the topic you are studying. The *Reader's Guide* is a summary of the contents of the most respected magazines and journals in the country. The *Reader's Guide* is available at just about every library, and it covers just about every topic of general interest, but it is considerably slower and less thorough than an informed search through a well designed online electronic reference system, which more and more libraries are offering these days. These systems will vary dramatically from library to library, but virtually all of them will ask you to provide a key word to begin the electronic search. Ask the librarian for help if you need it.

If you have affordable Internet access and are already familiar with the art of "surfing the Net," consider using this option as a *supplement* to your other study efforts. But beware: The Internet is a notorious time-consumer! If you're reading this book, odds are you don't have a lot of time to waste.

Nevertheless, if you're an experienced Net surfer, with a good sense of how to use key words to get information from a solid online reference source, set aside a short block of time, at about Step 7, to find online material that is relevant to your paper. Incorporate all the references and ideas on your cards. Cite each source completely in your bibliography in your paper's final draft.

Remember that your paper's opening paragraph is the most important part of all. The first paragraph in your paper sets out what you will be arguing for or against, and tells why you feel the way you do about the topic you're addressing. If it's well written, it will point the reader toward the rest of the paper and earn you points for solid organization. If it's poorly written, it may not matter what follows—your teacher may simply conclude that you don't know what you're talking about, and grade accordingly.

Take the time you need to develop a *superb* opening paragraph. Rewrite it as often as necessary to get it exactly right, then make sure the rest of the paper supports it.

Still having trouble? Take a look at Chapter 13. It's got essential advice on the most common ways to get around writer's block and tips on dealing with other problems you may be having in developing your report or paper.

Chapter 10

If your paper is due in 6 to 9 days

Okay, let's assume that you have eight days at your disposal to work on your paper, not counting the actual due date itself. What should you do when? Here's one possible breakdown that follows the 13-step plan outlined in Chapter 9. Use it as a model and be sure to use the scheduling tools we discussed in Chapter 2 to schedule your time intelligently.

Day 8: Determine the topic and "angle" of your paper. (Steps 1 through 3.)

Day 7: Develop a list of references. (Step 4.)

Days 6 to 4: Read your reference materials; take notes; compose your detailed outline; write your first draft. (Steps 5 and 6.)

Days 3 to 2: Do additional research if necessary; develop the second draft and edit the paper; prepare your bibliography/list of sources. (Steps 7 and 8.)

The day before your paper is due: Proofread the paper; print or type the final copy. (Steps 9 through 13.)

When you hit the library, ask the librarian to point you toward the *Reader's Guide to Periodical Literature;* use it to track down articles of interest.

Consider teaming up with a study partner. This is an option you may want to consider if you have only a week or so in which to compose a paper that must address a particularly daunting technical subject, or if you must develop a great deal of material from scratch in very short order. The idea is not to get the other person to write the paper for you, of course, but to use mutual brainstorming sessions to lead each of you toward ideas on your respective topics that you would not otherwise have come across.

If there's an appropriate person you can work with, preferably someone in the same class who's under the same time pressures you're under, you might want to give this a try for an hour or so and see what happens: Remember, however, that your aim is to develop two separate papers with two separate topics...not two papers that are carbon copies of one another! This idea may work best if you take one side of an argument as a central thesis for the paper and your study partner takes the other side of the issue.

Use the note cards you used to develop your detailed outline as inspiration for the text of your first draft. As I mentioned previously, those cards may be your best friend when it comes to developing the specific paragraphs and sentences of your paper. Use them to blow through creative roadblocks and other forms of writer's block.

Pay more attention to the first paragraph of your paper than to any other part. This is the part of the paper that sets out what you will be arguing for or against and why. As I have mentioned earlier, the opening paragraph is the section that makes the most difference to the teacher. It will probably have more impact on your grade than any other portion of the paper. Rewrite it as often as necessary to get it exactly right, then make sure the rest of the paper supports it.

Still having trouble? Take a look at Chapter 13. It's got some essential advice on the most common ways to get things moving in a positive direction.

Chapter 11

If your paper is due in 2 to 5 days

Let's say you have five days at your disposal to develop a great paper, not counting the day the paper is due. What should you do? Here's one possible schedule, based on the ideas outlined in Chapter 9. If you decide to adapt this schedule to your own needs, be sure to follow the steps laid out in Chapter 2.

Day 5: Determine the topic and "angle" of your paper. (Steps 1 through 3.)

Part of Day 4: Develop a list of references. (Step 4.)

Part of Day 4, all of Day 3: Read your reference materials; take notes; compose your detailed outline; write your first draft. (Steps 5 and 6.)

Days 2 and 1: Do additional research if necessary; develop the second draft and edit the paper; prepare your bibliography/list of sources. (Steps 7 and 8)

The day before your paper is due: Proofread the paper; print or type the final copy. (Steps 9 through 13.)

Consider teaming up with a study partner. As I mentioned in the previous chapter, this is an option you may want to consider if you have roughly a week in which to compose a particularly lengthy or complex paper from scratch. Be careful about how much time you devote to this technique; if it doesn't seem to be pointing you in the right direction almost immediately (after about an hour or so of discussion with your study partner), you should probably go back to working on your own.

This technique can be dangerous if it is misused! If you and your partner develop virtually identical approaches to virtually identical topics, you'll be wasting time and courting serious disciplinary action from the teacher. A better approach is to take *opposing* sides of an issue that will allow for a spirited, well-informed debate, and then use the results as a springboard for your 13-point paper-writing plan.

During your library research, check the *Reader's Guide to Periodical Literature* for appropriate article citations on the topic you are studying. As I noted earlier, the *Reader's Guide* is a summary of the contents of the most respected magazines and journals in the country. It can be an invaluable resource, whether you're trying to finalize your topic or looking for articles that support your thesis. It is especially helpful when you must gather research quickly.

Take a look at the note cards you used to develop your detailed outline. They can serve as great idea generators for the text of your first draft.

If you have to choose one part of your paper to pay particularly close attention to, that part should be your opening paragraph. This portion sets out exactly what you will be arguing; it's the chunk of the paper that matters the most to your instructor. Do as many rewrites as you have to to get this part of your paper exactly right—and then make sure the rest of your paper supports the argument you make in the opening paragraph. (If you finish reading your paper and realize that you've been proving the wrong side of the argument, there's a problem!)

If you find yourself stuck while trying to develop the text of your paper, you should turn to the appropriate section of Chapter 13 of this book. It's got some important advice on overcoming writer's block and dealing with other common problems related to paper-writing.

Chapter 12

If your paper is due *tomorrow*

WARNING: Last-minute paper-writing can be hazardous to your grade! I do not advise, condone or encourage putting off paper-writing until the 11th hour. Because of the amount of thought, research, organization, writing and review that such a task requires, it's important to set aside the time to do the job well.

But, you say, it's a little late for that advice now. Well, let's resort to some damage control. First of all, clear your calendar of all other responsibilities. You'll need to maximize every remaining waking hour.

The first step you must take is to plan your strategy! You really to need to take the time to sketch out a battle plan, even with only a day to get the job done. Your time is probably at more of a premium now than at any other time. It is imperative that you spend it wisely. I strongly recommend that you take 20 minutes to a half-hour to review the 13-step study plan outlined in Chapter 9. Then ask yourself the following questions:

- **Is there a way I can point this paper toward something I already know well enough to discuss comfortably?** Trying to get up to speed on material that is brand-new to you isn't the best way to develop a solid piece of research work or a superbly reasoned logical argument. Wherever possible, stick to what you know.

- **Is the central thesis—the argument I will try to prove or disprove in the paper—something that I feel passionately about? If not, should I think about selecting another one?** When it comes to developing a good deal of text in a short period of time, nothing beats writing about something that makes you mad, leaves you indignant or stokes your personal competitive fires. If you can pick a central thesis that touches strongly on something you have an emotional connection to, you may have won half the battle.
- **Are there two or three reliable research sources I can use to develop external sources of support, sources that I can cite for my argument?** These should ideally be *familiar* reference works or textbooks you either already possess or to which you have unrestricted, uncontested library access. At this stage of the game, it's not in your interest to waste valuable time trying to make sense of a book's organization or running around asking to borrow books from friends.

If you've taken a few moments to address these critical issues, you should be in a good position to create a back-of-the-envelope battle plan that touches on *all* or *most* of the essentials addressed in Chapter 9.

Here's one example of what such a one-day plan might look like. (Important note: If you plan to develop a good paper on anything like the accelerated schedule outlined here, you will almost certainly need to do so on a computer or word processor. Beg, borrow or liberate one in the nicest possible way, then get to work! If you have not worked with a computer or word processor before, then you should probably stick with the typewriter and find—or pay—someone who is willing to help you with the retyping and proofreading work.)

7:45 to 8 a.m: Eat breakfast! (A machine can't run without fuel!)

8 to 9:30 a.m: Schedule day; determine or reinforce topic and "angle" of your paper, with emphasis on topics of familiarity and/or strong emotional connection. (Steps 1 through 3.) Obtain two or three trusted reference resources. (Step 4.)

9:30 to 10:30 a.m: Review reference materials for key ideas; take notes; compose detailed outline. (Step 5.)

10:30 a.m. to 12:30 p.m: Write preliminary draft, leaving holes to fill in later. (Step 6.) Your aim here is to get a sense of the main points of your argument, not to put every comma in the right place!

12:30 to 1 p.m: *Eat lunch!* (Refueling and disengaging your mind for a brief time are essentials if you hope to get all the work done.)

1 to 4 p.m: Consult your reference sources for additional materials and inspiration. Develop a comprehensive draft; prepare your bibliography. (Steps 7 and 8.)

4 to 4:15 p.m: *Take a break!* (You can't expect to get detail-oriented work done if your brain is on "empty." Consider a healthy, high-energy snack.)

4:15 to 7 p.m: Continually review your paper for logical or grammatical problems and inconsistencies.

7 to 7:30 p.m: *Eat dinner!*

7:30 to 11 p.m: Proofread the paper; ask a friend to proofread it as well. Print or type the final copy. Be sure it is neat in appearance. (Steps 9 through 13.)

Don't work all night! If you try to compose your paper at 2 in the morning when you are exhausted, you will be betting your grade on your teacher's likelihood of mistaking gibberish for solid work. Don't chance it.

It's better to complete and turn in a short paper that actually makes sense than it is to stay up all night and pass in 20 pages of random notes that feature lots of grammatical and typographical errors. Do the best job you can within the time constraints available—or ask for an extension—but don't turn in a paper that looks like a stream-of-consciousness exercise.

Now that you've laid out your battle plan, take a moment to collect yourself. You've got a lot of work to do in a short period of time but don't let that rattle you. Stick with what you know, tell the truth and cite your sources. You'll be fine.

Pay more attention to the first paragraph of your paper than to any other part. This is the part of the paper that sets out what you will be arguing for or against and why. As I have mentioned earlier, the opening paragraph is the section that makes the most difference to the teacher. It will probably have more impact on your grade than any other portion of the paper. Rewrite it as often as necessary to get it exactly right, then make sure the rest of the paper supports it.

Review ideas in previous chapters of this book that may be helpful. In particular, you should take a look at Chapters 9 and 13 and use whatever seems appropriate to structure your paper, break through writer's block or overcome other issues you may be facing.

Chapter 13

Common questions on study strategy

Test-taking strategies

Q: If I have to guess, what's the best approach?

A: First instincts are probably the best ones to follow here—but *informed* first instincts are, of course, better still!

I'd advise you to keep one general rule of thumb in mind when trying to figure out *whether* to guess in the first place: When stymied while taking multiple-choice tests, you may want to guess when you can eliminate enough wrong answers to leave only two possible responses.

Q: Will I be penalized for guessing on tests?

A: This depends on the instructor and the test. If the teacher informs you that you'll earn three points for every correct answer but *lose* a point for every incorrect one, you may decide that leaving an answer blank is the best strategy if you really have no idea how to address a question. You may also want to think about how many potential responses you need to get out of the way before deciding that the odds will actually favor an inspired guess. If there is no penalty for wrong answers, you should probably avoid leaving an answer blank by eliminating wrong answers and working from the best two remaining options.

Q: What's the best way to approach true/false questions?

A: Here are some tricks to watch out for:

- Test-makers often incorporate two statements that *are* or *may be true* in a way that renders the *entire statement* false, often by implying a cause-and-effect relationship. Here's an example: "Because many automobiles get better gas mileage these days than the same models did 20 years ago, U.S. automakers have incorporated many passive-restraint safety systems in their vehicles." Each *half* of the statement is true, but the "because" implies that the first part causes the second. Watch out for these choices.
- The longer and more complicated an answer is, the less likely it is to be true, since *every* part of the statement has to be true for you to be correct in marking it so. This *doesn't* mean that every long sentence in a true-false test is false, but it does mean you should be awfully certain before placing a "T" answer next to a long-winded statement. (By the way, when it comes to *multiple choice* responses, the longest and most complicated answer is likeliest to be the most accurate one, because of the need to add qualifying statements. Again, this is not an iron-clad rule that will help you in every case, but a general principle to bear in mind when you come to a question you're not sure of.)
- Watch out for statements that prominently incorporate words like "none," "all," "never," "always" or "every." They may be subtle tipoffs that the answer in question should be marked "false." Very few absolute statements are true in every possible case.

Q: Suppose I finish early. Should I try to impress the teacher by handing the test in before anyone else does?

A: Absolutely not. Use *all* the time at your disposal. If you have extra time, *use* it to review your answers.

Q: How do I deal with essay questions?

A: Here's a five-step plan that will help:

1. Use a blank sheet of paper to *briefly* jot down facts, ideas and theories that you think have a place in your answer to the essay question. (If you've constructed a Power List that directly relates to the topic raised, this is an excellent time to reproduce it on paper, along with any other observations the essay question suggests to you.)
2. Now look at your notes and number them. Put a "1" by the idea you want to use first in answering the question; put a "2" by the idea you want to use second. Proceed quickly but thoroughly until you have placed a number by every idea you feel is worth incorporating in your essay answer.
3. Write your first paragraph. Spend as much time here as necessary to get the first paragraph absolutely right. *First paragraphs are where superior essay answers are made or unmade.* What is your position on the question raised? What are you arguing for or against? Why do you feel the way you do about the broad issue that has been opened for discussion?
4. Write the rest of your essay. Be sure it supports your first paragraph. Bear in mind that most teachers are impressed by accuracy and sound reasoning, rather than length.

5. Reread the essay. If you need to, make appropriate corrections and additions. Be sure to check for omissions that could have serious repercussions on the essay's readability (such as leaving out the word "not").

Report strategies

Q: Help! I tried your idea about using my outline cards for inspiration, and I still have writer's block! What do I do?

A: Here are some ideas that have proven successful for many other writers who've come up against this problem:

- Establish a pleasant reward that you *will* bestow upon yourself after you meet a certain goal. Maybe it's a party you've been invited to, an evening with a friend or a tempting piece of cheesecake that's waiting for you in your refrigerator. Whatever the reward you select for yourself, *fix* on it for a few moments, and then get started on the job at hand. If you get sidetracked, feel like procrastinating or start to spin your wheels, remind yourself of the reward that's awaiting you.
- Imagine that you're writing a letter to a good friend and trying to persuade him or her of the reasons you believe your thesis is correct.
- Developing a first draft? Don't edit as you go! Just get the words down. Worry about cutting and revising later. Sometimes the act of typing *something,* even something absurd, can help.
- Use simple language first. If you need to incorporate technical terms or proofs, do so later in the process. To get started, keep your writing basic and to the point, and don't trade up to the "dollar" words when the 25-cent ones will do.

- If you find yourself up against a roadblock, don't waste time on it. Come back later and try to resolve it. Keep going with some other part of your work. Often, you'll find that the change of "mental scenery" will be enough to help you resolve whatever was hanging you up earlier.

Q: I have an oral presentation to prepare, rather than a written report. Any suggestions?

A: Don't write a paper and read it word for word to your audience. You'll put everyone to sleep. Stick with 3 x 5 cards and develop a preliminary (then a detailed) outline, following the steps laid out earlier in this book.

Other points to bear in mind while preparing and delivering an oral report:

- **Keep the topic very specific.** This is great advice for written reports, too, but it's especially important when preparing a spoken presentation. If you're talking in generalities for 15 minutes, you're going to lose your instructor's interest, and you're not going to get a good grade. Stay away from topics like "The Theme of Death in Poetry." Instead, focus on something like "Death, Release and Redemption in the Later Poems of Sylvia Plath."

- **Practice!** The more you say your material *out loud* in the privacy of your own home, the more comfortable you'll be delivering it.

- **Use a *brief*, humorous, pertinent anecdote or quote early on in the presentation.** There is something to be said for getting a chuckle during the first minute or two of your presentation. Attribute the source.

- **Go easy on the statistics.** Don't spend any more time than you have to spouting numbers at people.
- **Pick one person in the group to talk to.** Think of your talk as a one-on-one conversation, not an address to the nation from the Oval Office.

Q: I'm really *up against the wall schedule-wise. Is it okay if I skip the step where I track down someone else to read my paper?*

A: No! When it comes to getting good grades from teachers, neatness and accuracy definitely count. Checking for correct spelling and grammar count more when the material you're developing is being assembled at the last minute. There are a lot of factors working against you now (time, for instance); you must make absolutely certain that the way your teacher perceives the paper's physical appearance and writing quality isn't one of those factors.

Do whatever it takes to secure a second pair of eyes to go over your paper before you hand it in. Be sure that the version of the paper you hand in is error-free. Perhaps just as important, be sure that your paper *looks* sharp. It should be clean, neatly bound, clipped or stapled, and free of wrinkles and stains. It should *always* be typewritten or printed, *never* handwritten.

Conclusion

In this book, you've learned about the best strategies for getting a whole lot of study work done in a short period of time. I hope the ideas have been helpful...and I also hope you don't have to make a habit of appealing to them.

If your study work regularly features "down-to-the-wire" work on projects like paper-writing and test preparation, there's a good chance your whole time management approach could stand some improvement. While it's certainly true that many people get their best work done under pressure, it's also true that pushing yourself to the outer reaches of deadlines time and again, for test after test and paper after paper, isn't much fun. The fact is, if you deal with *everything* at the last minute, your grades won't be as good as they should be. And that's a shame.

Before we close this book, I'd like to offer some amplifying thoughts that will help you make good long-term time management a permanent reality in your study work:

- *Tackle the tough stuff first.* You know that important part of your study work you really aren't looking forward to doing? Put it at the top of the list and don't move on to the next item until you've completed it. Reward yourself for a job well done once you wrap that first item up. If you approach your study work in this way, I guarantee that you'll have fewer problems as your deadline draws near.

- *Make your schedule specific.* Don't write the word "study" in that big three-hour block of time you've set aside. Keep your goal specific; something like "Read the first three acts of *Measure for Measure.*"
- *Remember to write everything down.* Write down everything related to scheduling in your Study Plan Central book. Jot down study ideas and connections the moment you think of them in your class notebook. You'll avoid the "information overload syndrome" that can make study work so stressful.
- *Figure out how to manage distractions—or yield to them for a while.* Find a way to set appropriate limits and focus with full concentration on the task at hand. If that's not possible, *continue with your study work until you reach a natural stopping point,* then note where you left off and take a break.
- *Don't skip around.* Identify one important goal at a time. Keep at it until you've hit the mark you set for yourself. Sure, you may want to get a look at the important elements of a number of different areas of your topic. Do that. But make a list of what you want to accomplish in each area and don't move on until you've attained the first goal.
- *Follow your own rhythms.* Some of us can sit down for hours at a time to review study materials; others are more comfortable with lots of little bursts of planned, high-energy activity. Find your own style.
- *Use all the planning forms and strategies included in this book.* Take advantage of them!

Here's hoping your short-term and long-term study efforts turn out work that's as sharp as it can possibly be. Congratulations on committing to a sound, ongoing time management routine!

For further reference

"Ace" Any Test, 3rd ed., Ron Fry, Career Press, Franklin Lakes, NJ, 1996.

How to Study, 4th ed., Ron Fry, Career Press, Franklin Lakes, NJ, 1996.

Improve Your Memory, 3rd ed., Ron Fry, Career Press, Franklin Lakes, NJ, 1996.

Manage Your Time, 2nd ed., Ron Fry, Career Press, Franklin Lakes, NJ, 1994.

The Memory Book, Harry Lorayne and Jerry Lucas, Stein and Day, New York, 1974.

Improve Your Writing, 3rd ed., Ron Fry, Career Press, Franklin Lakes, NJ, 1996.

About the author

Ron Fry has edited or written more than 30 books, including the best-selling *How to Study* series, *101 Great Answers to the Toughest Interview Questions*, *Your First Interview*, *Your First Resume* and *Your First Job*.

He is an acknowledged authority, frequent speaker and seminar leader on a variety of educational topics at schools and associations nationwide.

Index